ASSESSMENT IN THE BLOCK: THE LINK TO INSTRUCTION

Laura L. McCullough

Brenda M. Tanner

EYE ON EDUCATION

EYE ON EDUCATION
6 DEPOT WAY WEST, SUITE 106
LARCHMONT, NY 10538
(914) 833–0551
(914) 833–0761 fax
www.eyeoneducation.com

Library of Congress Cataloging-in-Publication Data

McCullough, Laura L., 1954–
    Assessment in the block : the link to instruction / Laura L. McCullough and Brenda M. Tanner.
    p. cm. — (Teaching in the block)
    Includes bibliographical references.
    ISBN 1-930556-07-1
    1. Educational tests and measurements. 2. Education—Evaluation. 3. Block scheduling (Education) I. Tanner, Brenda M., 1953– II. Title. III. Series.

    LB3051.M46246   2001
    371.26—dc21

                               00-063603

10 9 8 7 6 5 4 3 2 1

Editorial and production services provided by
Richard H. Adin Freelance Editorial Services
52 Oakwood Blvd., Poughkeepsie, NY 12603-4112
(845-471-3566)

Other EYE ON EDUCATION *Books on Block Scheduling*

Also Available from EYE ON EDUCATION

Coaching and Mentoring First-Year and Student Teachers
by India Podsen and Vicki Denmark

**Staff Development: Practices that Promote
Leadership in Learning Communities**
by Sally J. Zepeda

Writing in the Content Areas
by Amy Benjamin

Performance Standards and Authentic Learning
by Allan A. Glatthorn

**Performance Assessment and Standards-Based Curricula:
The Achievement Cycle**
by Allan A. Glatthorn

Best Practices from America's Middle Schools
by Charles R. Watson

**The Performance Assessment Handbook
Volume 1: Portfolios and Socratic Seminars
Volume 2: Performances and Exhibitions**
by Bil Johnson

**The School Portfolio: A Comprehensive Framework
for School Improvement 2nd ed.**
by Victoria L. Bernhardt

Data Analysis for Comprehensive Schoolwide Improvement
by Victoria L. Bernhardt

Designing and Using Databases for School Improvement
by Victoria L. Bernhardt

The Example School Portfolio
by Victoria L. Bernhardt

Research on Educational Innovations, 2nd ed.
by Arthur K. Ellis and Jeffrey T. Fouts

Personalized Instruction: Changing Classroom Practice
by James Keefe and John Jenkins

**Banishing Anonymity:
Middle and High School Advisement Programs**
by John Jenkins and Bonnie Daniel

**Collaborative Learning in Middle and Secondary Schools:
Applications and Assessments**
by Dawn Snodgrass and Mary Bevevino

**English Teacher's Guide to Performance Tasks
and Rubrics: Middle School**
by Amy Benjamin

**English Teacher's Guide to Performance Tasks
and Rubrics: High School**
by Amy Benjamin

**Performance-Based Learning and Assessment
in Middle School Science**
by K. Michael Hibbard

**Developing Parent and Community Understanding
of Performance-Based Assessment**
by Kathryn Anderson Alvestad

A Collection of Performance Tasks and Rubrics

Middle School Mathematics
by Charlotte Danielson

High School Mathematics
by Charlotte Danielson and Elizabeth Marquez

High School English Teacher's Guide to Active Learning
by Victor Moeller and Marc Moeller

Middle School English Teacher's Guide to Active Learning
by Marc Moeller and Victor Moeller

Directory of Programs for Students at Risk
by Thomas L. Williams

The Interdisciplinary Curriculum
by Arthur K. Ellis and Carol J. Stuen

**The Paideia Classroom:
Teaching for Understanding**
by Terry Roberts with Laura Billings

ABOUT THE AUTHORS

Laura L. McCullough currently serves as principal of Stone-Robinson School in Albemarle County, Virginia. She has taught at the elementary, middle, high school, undergraduate, and graduate school levels, and has worked as a staff development facilitator and a math/science specialist in Virginia schools. Through the University of Virginia, Laura teaches assessment courses and workshops in a variety of schools and districts. She earned her Ed.D. degree from the University of Virginia.

Brenda M. Tanner currently serves as Chief Academic Officer for the Horry County Public Schools in South Carolina. Previously, she directed a professional development consortium for the University of Virginia, working with the Curry School of Education and 20 Virginia school divisions. She has more than 20 years of experience as a teacher, staff developer, administrator, and assistant professor. She earned her Ed.D. degree from the University of Virginia and has written and consulted on block scheduling, performance standards, and other related topics.

FOREWORD

Block schedules provide opportunities for teachers to change their instructional strategies so that students become more active and successful learners. There is a growing body of evidence from experiences with high school and middle school scheduling that strongly supports the notion that with proper staff development and careful schedule design the overall school environment becomes more positive and productive. There also is evidence that many teachers increase their personal contacts with students. Furthermore, when curricular and instructional issues are addressed appropriately, achievement in many schools improves, as measured by factors such as reduced failure rates, increased numbers of students on honor rolls, and higher test scores.

Because we believe that instructional change is the key to successful block scheduling, we are sponsoring this series of books, written primarily by teachers who have been successful in teaching in block schedules. While we believe this series can be helpful to teachers working in any type of schedule, the ideas should be especially useful for middle and high school teachers who are "teaching in the block."

The idea of scheduling middle and high schools in some way other than daily, single periods is not new. We find in educational history numerous attempts to modify traditional schedules and to give the instructional school day greater flexibility. In the 1960s, for example, approximately 15 percent of American high schools implemented modular scheduling, which typically used 15 to 20 modules of time to create instructional periods that varied in length from between 15 minutes to classes of 100 minutes or more.

Many reasons have been given for the demise of modular scheduling as practiced during the 1960s and 1970s; however, two of the primary reasons often cited (Canady and Rettig, 1995, pp. 13–15) are that (a) too much independent study time was included in those schedules and school management became a problem, and (b) teachers in many schools never were assisted in seriously changing classroom instruction in longer periods of time. Current models of block scheduling do not have significant independent study time; therefore, school management problems are reduced, not exacerbated. We have found, however, that in schools where block scheduling has been implemented successfully, considerable attention has been paid to adapting instruction to maximize the potential of available time.

We repeatedly have stated that if schools only "change their bells" block scheduling should not be implemented. We also have contended that if teachers are not provided with extensive staff development, block scheduling will be a problem. "The success or failure of the [current] block scheduling movement will be determined largely by the ability of teachers…to improve instruction. Regardless of a school's time schedule, what happens between individual teachers and students in classrooms is still most important, and simply altering the manner in which we schedule schools will not ensure better instruction by teachers or increased learning by students"(Canady and Rettig, 1995, p. 240).

In this sixth volume of our *Teaching in the Block* series, entitled *Assessment in the Block: The Link to Instruction,* authors Laura L. McCullough and Brenda M. Tanner offer specific strategies for connecting instruction to assessment and showing how a block schedule enhances the process. In addition to their building-level and central office administrative experiences, in their combined 50+ years in education, they have taught at the elementary, middle, high school, and college levels.

Laura and Brenda contend that the organization of the school day influences the delivery of instruction and the methods of assessing student learning. Block scheduling provides opportunities for teachers to redesign instructional and assessment methods in order to increase the level of student involvement in the learning process. With longer blocks of instructional time comes the opportunity for teachers to use a wider range of instructional and assessment strategies in their classrooms. For example, they illustrate how instructional and assessment opportunities are expanded in block schedules; how teachers are more likely to act as facilitators rather than directors of learning; and how students are more likely to participate in a variety of assessments and instructional activities rather than sit as mere recipients of knowledge.

This book is a useful guide for all teachers working in this age of accountability. It is especially helpful to upper elementary, middle, and high school teachers working in extended periods of time simply because longer time blocks allow for expanded assessment and instructional possibilities.

The authors give concrete examples and illustrations from many disciplines. Their goal is for teachers to use various assessments and a range of instructional methods that will engage students and involve them in the learning process. Just as teachers should employ a variety of instructional strategies in teaching, so should students' responses reflect multiple ways of learning. This book is a practical resource for instructors who are *assessing and teaching* in the block. We highly recommend it.

Robert Lynn Canady
Michael D. Rettig

TABLE OF CONTENTS

1

BLOCK SCHEDULES AND CLASSROOM ASSESSMENT: THE CONNECTION

Time is a factor that influences the decisions we make. School schedules divide the day into parcels of instructional time. Teachers design instructional programs that are packaged for these allotted time periods. In secondary schools, this traditionally has meant that teaching practices have been limited to those that fit into a class period of 45 minutes or less. Given the time needed for transitions and for administrative duties, instructional time often has been reduced to 30 minutes or less.

As time for instruction has been limited, so, too, has the time for assessment of student learning. Faced with limited class time, little planning or preparation time, and student loads of more than 100, teachers often resort to controlled-response tests or quizzes as the primary method of evaluating student learning. These multiple-choice, true/false, or fill-in-the-blank assessments reduce the time for test taking and scoring by restricting the responses available to students. Traditional tests such as these serve to evaluate the students' general knowledge of the content. Successes are measured by the students' abilities to memorize facts and procedures and apply them in a very controlled setting. In such testing situations, students have little or no opportunity to respond critically to information, to apply knowledge or skills, or to create new structures.

That students must be prepared to take standardized tests cannot be denied. Development of national and state standards spurred an emphasis on accountability and, in turn, an emphasis on standardized tests. As part of the college admissions process, students spend many hours preparing for and responding to tests presented in the multiple-choice format. In the midst of all these testing requirements, adolescents perhaps await most eagerly the test that measures their knowledge of the rules of the road. This test receives no letter grade or stanine score that requires interpretation, but when scored, it has immediate and understandable implications for the test-taker.

We acknowledge the importance of standardized measures of student achievement as well as the need to provide instruction in basic test-taking strategies. However, our purpose is not to discuss standardized testing programs, but to focus on issues related to classroom assessment. More specifically, we will discuss a range of assessment strategies. We will recommend strategies that we believe promote learning and yield high-quality assessment information. We do not attempt to provide a recipe for classroom assessment, but we do hope to stimulate thought and to provide practical suggestions for the classroom teacher.

Of course, we recognize that good assessment is good assessment, no matter what the schedule. However, the extended class periods provided in a block schedule create a context in which these assessment strategies can be most powerful. The block schedule facilitates the use of high-quality assessments by providing the extended time that students need to fully engage in sophisticated, complex tasks.

Assessment strategies need to vary to match the objectives of instruction. Teachers who want to encourage students to apply what they have learned and challenge students to extend their learning past the controlled classroom environment need multiple measures of student achievement. Just as those who measure a student's ability to operate a motor vehicle rely on a test of knowledge *and* an assessment of performance, so, too, should teachers strive to employ a variety of assessment strategies. Anyone who has prepared a gourmet meal, assembled a swing set, built a structure, or facilitated a committee meeting can attest to the fact that there is definitely a difference between knowing what to do and actually completing the task successfully. We will discuss the difference between *knowing* and *doing* and provide suggestions for methods to measure the two.

Whether the focus is on assessing knowledge or evaluating performance, we believe that high-quality assessments serve not only as measurement tools, but also as learning tools. That is, meaningful and challenging assessment tasks become opportunities for student learning. Most students are accustomed to classrooms in which instruction and assessment are mutually exclusive. A cycle of teaching and learning occurs, and then stops so that the assessment can take place. In general, we do not think of teaching or learning as things that happen during a test. In this book, however, we challenge teachers to consider that in many cases, assessment of student learning can *and should* occur during learning time. We demonstrate that even cumulative assessments, such as those that occur at the end of units or semesters, can be designed so that students can demonstrate what they know while continuing to learn.

TIME FOR CHANGE

Teachers and administrators have begun to recognize the significant impact of the daily schedule on the instructional program. The limitations of traditional schedules are being realized as educators explore instructional models that require students to combine content knowledge with critical-thinking skills. Class schedules are being redesigned to accommodate the need for time to involve students in the construction of knowledge, rather than limiting their participation to note taking and the reading of textbooks. Block scheduling provides models for reorganizing the school day and the school year to maximize the use of instructional time. Instead of segmenting the day into six or seven

45-minute periods, block scheduling models divide the day into fewer periods that provide extended time for instruction.

Canady and Rettig (1995) use the following points to accentuate the influence of scheduling on the instructional program:

♦ A schedule can be viewed as a *resource;* it is the schedule that permits the *effective utilization of people, space, time and resources* in an organization.

♦ A schedule can help *solve problems* related to the *delivery of instruction;* or a schedule can be a major source of problems.

♦ A schedule can facilitate the institutionalization of desired programs and instructional practices. (p. 29)

Teachers who are asked to work together in teams need common planning periods in order to develop integrated units, examine student work, meet with resource teachers, and confer with parents. Students who are asked to tackle projects and to explore concepts need uninterrupted blocks of time for their work. Block schedules can provide teachers and students with the time they need to focus on instruction.

TIME FOR INSTRUCTION

As schools have adopted block schedules, teachers have adapted to the rearrangement of instructional periods by changing their instructional methods and strategies. In the article "New Class on the Block," Day (1995) speaks of the benefits of block scheduling for science teachers: "In one 90-minute period, the teachers can introduce or reinforce a major concept, incorporate an experimental or research activity to enhance the concept, and still have time for follow-up activities or discussions that provide closure" (p. 28). Gerking (1995) writes of the rearrangement of instruction to allow for more group work and activities. Teachers working in a block schedule spend less time lecturing as they incorporate technology to "reinforce concepts and help involve all students in the material" (p. 23).

Salvaterra and Adams (1995) report changes in the instructional programs of two northeastern Pennsylvania schools with restructured schedules. Opportunities for class trips, cooperative learning projects, computer and science lab work, and research are noted. Extended class time is seen as an opportunity for "teachers to delve deeply into concepts" (p. 32).

The implementation of block scheduling has resulted in teachers incorporating a greater variety of instructional strategies into their lessons. When asked to identify changes that had occurred in their teaching as a result of block scheduling, a group of high school teachers identified an increase in the following strategies and activities (Tanner, 1996):

♦ Active inquiry

♦ Cooperative learning

- Discovery learning
- Hands-on activities
- Off-campus trips
- Projects
- Research
- Role play
- Simulations
- Student presentations
- Technology usage
- Writing

The extended periods of time provided by block scheduling offer teachers the opportunity to move from a "teacher as expert" model to one in which the teacher becomes the facilitator of student learning. In this model, the goal of the teacher is to utilize instructional methods that will engage the students and involve them in the learning process. Expectations for student learning behaviors change. Rather than recipients of knowledge imparted by the teacher, students are expected to be participants who are actively engaged in the learning process. Figure 1.1 lists a number of teaching strategies that involve and engage students in different ways. We invite teachers to use the list to examine their instructional practices and to consider the implications these practices have for the assessment of student learning.

Goodlad (1994) argues that instead of turning our students into "answer-getters," we, as educators, should help them to "learn how to learn." As part of this learning process, students should be involved in a variety of activities. "Students should not be taught *a* way of knowing. They should have encounters with many ways through many different kinds of media, and they should develop a repertoire of approaches" (p. 113). According to Goodlad, students should be provided with a variety of "means" to use as they learn to "grapple with" concepts. These means include "reading and writing,…dancing, drawing, constructing, touching, thinking, talking, shaping, [and] planning" (p. 113). Just as teachers should employ a variety of instructional strategies in teaching, so should students' responses reflect multiple ways of learning.

FIGURE 1.1. WHAT'S MY INSTRUCTIONAL STYLE?

We all have unique styles of teaching. Think of the lessons you plan and the types of activities you use to support the lesson. Use the following checklist as a tool to reflect on your instructional practices.

Instructional Strategies	Often Use	Seldom Use	Never Use
Concept Attainment			
Concept Development			
Cooperative Learning			
Demonstrations			
Experiments			
Field/Study Trips			
Inquiry			
Integrated Technology			
Investigations			
Learning Centers			
Lecture/Presentation			
Manipulatives			
Memory Models			
Research Activities			
Simulations			
Socratic Seminars			
Synectics			
Textbook Readings and Questions			
Other			

For more information on the instructional strategies listed above, teachers should consult Canady and Rettig's *Teaching in the Block: Strategies for Engaging Active Learners* and *Instruction, a Models Approach,* by Gunter, Estes, and Schwab.

TIME FOR ASSESSMENT

As expectations for students' involvement in the learning process change, so, too, should the methods for assessing students' learning. Multiple-choice and true/false tests will not suffice when the goal is to assess such things as the students' understanding of scientific methods, their skill in using graphing calculators, or their ability to debate key historical issues. In *High School Restructuring: A National Study* (1994), Cawelti examined the use of alternative assessment techniques as part of eight elements of curriculum/teaching restructuring:

> A standardized test of grammar bears little relationship to a student's ability to write well, and a multiple-choice science test does not measure a student's ability to apply modes of scientific reasoning to a laboratory experiment. In response to the need for better assessment, high schools are developing assessment plans that call for portfolios, projects, and other demonstrations of what teachers believe is important for students to know about a specific subject or skills area. (p. 13)

The issue of how to assess student learning should not be reduced to an "either/or" debate or a ranking according to value. What should be considered is the importance of examining the curriculum in order to determine what it is that students should *know* and be able to *do* and to make assessment decisions based upon these goals and objectives.

Remember the pressure you felt when taking a timed test? Did some of your energy and attention go into watching the clock rather than answering the questions? In a sense, any test that we take or any assessment in which we are involved is timed. Time provides boundaries within which we must function. As schedules have changed and extended periods of class time have been created, the boundaries surrounding instruction and assessment have expanded. Rushing through an assignment in order to complete it within a 45-minute period is a thing of the past. Teachers who may have avoided the use of performance assessments because they did not want to end the period with incomplete work may be encouraged by knowing that the block schedule provides extended periods of time for task completion. (See Figure 1.2.)

An increased opportunity to involve students in the assessment process is another benefit of extended classroom periods. How often have you heard students ask, "Why do we have to learn this?" Or, have you ever heard the collective sigh when an assignment is distributed, followed by the perennial question, "Will this be graded?" Students constantly question the relevancy of the curriculum and the importance of assignments and tests. When assessment methods are expanded, students are provided opportunities to demonstrate their knowledge and use their skills in a variety of ways. Presentations, performances or constructions are tasks that are more likely to engage the students because they are purposeful.

FIGURE 1.2. TRADITIONAL VS. BLOCK SCHEDULE

When students must start and stop their work every 45 minutes, the range of assessment strategies is restricted. Block scheduling provides extended periods of time for students to be involved in tasks, such as exhibitions, that require more thinking and action than that which can be measured on a fill-in-the-blank test. Sizer (1992) describes the use of an exhibition as a means for a student to "exhibit the products of his learning." The experience is described as the "academic equivalent of being able to sink free throws in basketball."

> To shoot baskets well one needs to practice. To think well one needs to practice. Going to school is practicing to use one's mind well. One does not exercise one's mind in a vacuum; one rarely learns to "think" well with nothing but tricky brainteasers or questions embedded in a context that is neither realistic nor memorable. One needs to stimulate its exercise with engaging ideas in an equally engaging setting. Such ideas require the grasp of fundamental information. (pp. 25–26)

The emphasis here is on the *use* of knowledge. As Sizer points out, the effective use of knowledge is much more complex than the recall of facts, rules, or procedures. Using ideas actually solidifies the learning process, serving as "a vehicle for fixing" the information and skills into the mind of the learner.

Teachers working in block schedules have more time to involve students in self-evaluations. Students often equate assessment with an end-of-the-unit test that is given one day and returned the next as a red-inked document. In the eyes of the students, these tests signal that a cycle of learning has ended. Teachers make judgments and give grades; students see themselves as removed from the evaluation process. With expanded classroom periods, teachers have time to discuss questions and to clarify misunderstandings as part of the re-teaching process. When teachers begin to expand their repertoire of assessment strategies to include performance tasks, they need to establish clear expectations for student performance. Students can and should be involved in the development and maintenance of checklists and rubrics used to monitor their progress. In doing this, students have the continual opportunity to compare their work to a defined target.

We suggest that the organization of the school day influences decisions about the delivery of instruction *and* the methods of assessing student learning. Block scheduling provides opportunities for teachers to redesign instructional and assessment methods in order to increase the level of student involvement in the learning process. With longer periods of time comes the opportunity for teachers to use a wider range of instructional and assessment strategies in their classrooms. (See Figure 1.3.)

FIGURE 1.3. INSTRUCTIONAL AND ASSESSMENT METHODS

Traditional Schedule	*Block Schedule*
• Instructional and assessment opportunities are limited.	• Instructional and assessment opportunities are expanded.
• Teachers tend to act as directors of learning.	• Teachers are more likely to act as facilitators of learning.
• Students tend to act as recipients of knowledge.	• Students are more likely to participate in a variety of instructional activities.

Block scheduling provides time for a *balanced* approach to assessment. Teachers taking this approach vary their assessment strategies just as they vary their instructional practices. Applying a range of assessment options, they match assessment to instruction as they examine student learning.

2

INSTRUCTION AND
ASSESSMENT:
THE CONNECTION

LINKING CURRICULUM, INSTRUCTION, AND ASSESSMENT

Too frequently, educators think about instruction and assessment as two separate issues. Many of us learned to think this way as preservice and beginning teachers, who were required to *first* develop an objective, *then* design an activity to accompany it, and *then* figure out a way to assess whether students had met the objective. This planning process is represented by the sequence of steps shown in Figure 2.1.

FIGURE 2.1. TRADITIONAL PLANNING PROCESS

Curriculum   ⟶   **Instruction**   ⟶   **Assessment**

This linear process begins with the content, or the "what," of instruction, moves to the strategies, or the "how," of teaching, and concludes with an assessment of student learning. Generally, when this model is transferred into classroom practice, the major actor is the teacher, who presents the unit, stops teaching to assess what's been learned, then scores and returns the test. The danger here is that students may be passive recipients of instruction and grades, rather than active participants in learning and assessment.

Those who insist that assessment should drive instruction propose an alternative planning model. "Begin with the end in mind" is a popular phrase. This view, represented in Figure 2.2, suggests that we design the assessment and share it with students first, setting an established target toward which lessons and units are aimed.

FIGURE 2.2. AN ALTERNATIVE PLANNING MODEL

Curriculum ⟶ **Assessment** ⟶ **Instruction**

For teachers, this process requires a very different way of thinking. For students, it makes the objective clear. When teachers and students have a shared understanding of what they are working toward, they are more likely to achieve the goal.

Although the alternative planning model has some advantages over the traditional planning model, it still links curriculum, assessment, and instruction in a step-by-step, sequential process. Like the traditional planning model, the alternative planning model has a distinctive beginning, middle, and end.

These step-by-step approaches appear to work for *teachers*, but we're not convinced that they are in the best interests of students. Where, we wonder, does the *learner* fit? How do these models accommodate students with diverse and changing instructional needs? In classrooms in which teachers are taking advantage of larger blocks of time to involve students in more student-directed, complex, and engaging instructional activities, should not assessment be *part* of the process?

We suggest that teachers think about linking curriculum with instruction and assessment in a more dynamic planning model that answers the need for continuous feedback to and from students. This does not mean that instruction is not goal-oriented or that learning targets are not clear. It *does* mean that teachers use various kinds of feedback to *continually* assess student learning during instruction (we have some practical suggestions for doing this in Chapter 3). It also means that when the time comes for summative assessment (at the end of a unit or semester, for example), learning does not have to come to a screeching halt so that assessment can begin. Rather, the assessment itself can be designed in ways that promote further student learning.

From our experience working with teachers, we know that setting goals, delivering instruction, and assessing learning rarely occur in a linear, sequential process. Particularly as teachers gain experience and sophistication in the planning process, they make instructional and assessment decisions in less linear, more complex ways. During their planning processes, expert teachers generate a range of instructional and assessment ideas. Then they begin narrowing down and revising these ideas, weaving instruction and assessment together in ways that support student learning of curricular goals. This more dynamic view of planning actually represents an important premise of good assessment, which is that *assessment reflects and is embedded in instruction*. The process of planning a unit of instruction should reflect this natural integration of teaching and assessing. That is, teaching, learning, and assessing can take place simultaneously.

In this context, assessment does not drive instruction, nor does instruction drive assessment. Rather, instruction and assessment are integrated into one seamless process, in which *both* are driven by meaningful, challenging, and authentic goals.

- By *meaningful*, we mean that there is some connection or "hook" that engages and interests students.
- By *challenging*, we mean that students are involved in activities that require them to apply thinking and process skills in order to understand and make sense of what they're learning.
- By *authentic*, we mean that students are learning how skills and content relate to real-world contexts and issues.

Our version of the model, shown in Figure 2.3, views planning as a dynamic process, a process that continuously interweaves curriculum, instruction, and assessment. Planning for one part of the instructional process necessitates the consideration of all areas. Instruction and assessment go hand in hand, supporting and complementing each other. Activities that show teachers what and how students are learning (that is, assessment activities) are ongoing, and become part of the daily instructional practice in the classroom.

FIGURE 2.3. DYNAMIC PLANNING MODEL

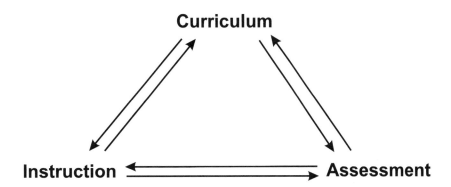

This model represents a more integrated approach to planning, and shows that assessment is ongoing, not a single event at the end of each unit.

CLARIFYING INSTRUCTIONAL GOALS

The first priority for teachers planning instruction is to *clarify the instructional goals*. Teachers often do not develop goals themselves; instead, goals come from state standards and various curriculum guides and textbooks. Many of these goals are not terribly specific, and, therefore, are open to interpretation by teachers translating them into lessons and units. For example, one of the Virginia Standards of Learning (Commonwealth of Virginia, 1995) for tenth graders states: "The student will use maps, globes, photographs, and pictures to analyze the physical and human landscapes of the world in order to identify regional climatic patterns and weather phenomena and relate them to events in the contemporary world." A teacher reading this goal is unlikely to know where to begin without considerable thought about what the goal really means. Teachers might ask themselves:

- What are the "big ideas" or most important understandings here? (For a complete discussion about identifying essential understandings, see Wiggins and McTighe, 1998.)
- What are the facts that must be learned as a basis for building these broad understandings?
- What skills should students gain as we work toward this goal together?
- What essential skills (those with broad application across units) are part of this unit?

Various teachers may answer these questions in different ways. This is probably unavoidable, and may, in fact, be desirable. The translation of broad goals into classroom practice is part of the art of teaching. Still, each individual teacher must be clear about his or her interpretation of the goal. Otherwise, learning targets and expectations may be ambiguous to students, and instruction will not be clear and focused.

We suggest two alternative ways for teachers to think about clarifying goals. The first is a tool that we call an "unpacking chart." This graphic organizer helps teachers analyze broad goals and look at their component parts. This "unpacking" is similar to a task analysis, though more complex. The second framework for clarifying goals is Bloom's *Taxonomy*, which is already familiar to most classroom teachers. We believe that teachers can use the taxonomy as an instrument for translating broad goals into focused instructional plans and activities.

UNPACKING INSTRUCTIONAL GOALS

Unpacking instructional goals helps teachers look analytically at their instructional objectives in order to articulate exactly what is to be learned. This process enables teachers to link instructional and assessment strategies closely to curricular goals, and facilitates the dynamic relationship that we have described.

The process of unpacking a goal assists the teacher in

♦ Assessing students' prior knowledge;

♦ Choosing teaching methods that target the kinds of learning necessary to meet the goal; and

♦ Setting criteria for the assessment to describe the successful attainment of the goal.

To choose the best instructional and assessment tools for the job, teachers must clarify the combination of content and skills they wish students to learn. Some goals are highly "content-loaded"; others clearly focus on the development of a skill. Thoughtful teachers often combine content and skill objectives into challenging tasks for students. These tasks require students to use the content they know and apply their skills in an integrated, real way. For examples, see Figure 2.4.

FIGURE 2.4. COMBINING CONTENT AND SKILLS

A highly content-loaded objective:

Name the generals of the Civil War and tell with which army they fought.

An objective for a skill:

Given data, students will find the range, mean, median, and mode.

A task which combines skill and content objectives:

Make a scale drawing of a building that is highly energy efficient. Label the characteristics of the building that are specifically designed to conserve energy and describe how they work. *Here, students are required to apply scale drawing (a **skill** objective) and combine it with knowledge they have gained about energy use (a **content** objective) in order to complete to task.*

To choose assessments and design lessons that effectively target the desired learning, we use an "unpacking chart" (Figure 2.5). This graphic organizer helps teachers think analytically about curricular goals in order to make them clear and explicit.

FIGURE 2.5. UNPACKING CHART

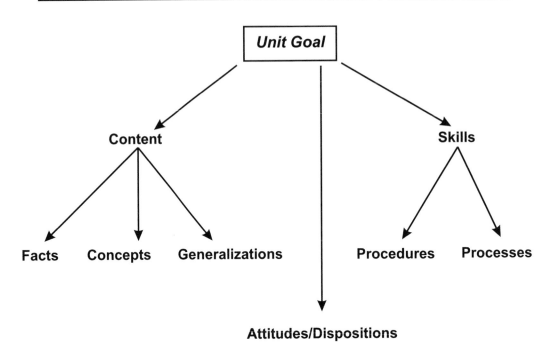

Using the unpacking chart, we ask teachers to think about *content* as that which they want students to *know*. Within the category of content, we discuss:

♦ *Facts.* Facts are pieces of knowledge; statements that are known to be true. "The sassafras tree has leaves of three different shapes" and "Annapolis is the capital of Maryland" are facts. When we are teaching students facts, we are increasing the breadth of their basic knowledge about the world.

♦ *Concepts.* Concepts are ideas that people interpret, picture, or imagine. When we are teaching students concepts, we are building and deepening their understanding. Students of different ages might have very different understandings of a concept such as "flower." For a young child, the concept is simple. A flower grows on a plant, is colorful, and often smells nice. As students mature, they learn about the variety of flowers and about wild versus propagated flowers. They use "flower" as a verb, and then as a metaphor for an awakening or maturation. The concept continues to develop and the understanding to deepen. We also study concepts that are much more abstract to begin with, such as the concept of justice, the concept of war or the concept of a billion.

♦ *Generalizations.* Generalizations link concepts together and describe their relationships. For example, "the planets revolve in elliptical orbits" is a generalization that involves the concepts of planets, revolution, orbit, and ellipse. A misunderstanding or insufficient understanding of any of these concepts impairs the student's ability to understand and work with the generalization.

The *skills* section of the unpacking chart contains those things that we want students to be able to *do*. Within the skills category, it is useful to delineate procedures and processes as types of skills calling for different types of teaching and assessment.

♦ *Procedures.* When students are mastering a procedure, they primarily are learning to remember and apply a series of steps. Although the steps may not always occur in the same sequence or appear in exactly the same form, they are reasonably recognizable and consistent. Solving an algebraic equation, creating a bar graph to represent a data set, and taking a blood pressure reading are examples of procedures.

♦ *Processes.* Processes are those types of skills that educators often call "problem solving" or "thinking skills." These skills involve thinking that goes beyond procedures to include the creation of new ideas by students, the manipulation or combination of ideas in unique ways, or the connection of new content to students' experience, prior learning, and/or system of values. When students develop arguments for a debate, generate hypotheses, or role-play the conversation that two historical figures might have had with each other, they are using process skills.

The conversation among educators regarding the teaching of *attitudes and dispositions* (sometimes called "values") has taken various twists and turns in recent decades. Without engaging in the "values education" debate, it is safe to say that there are certain attitudes and dispositions that help students succeed in school. The most obvious is probably the disposition to be a learner. Students who are interested in and curious about new knowledge learn more, and they learn it more easily. In science, we hope students will develop some degree of skepticism, which will cause them to seek proof of and demand justification for generalizations. In government, we seek to teach students to value the democratic process, and to take seriously their responsibilities as citizens. Across all grades and content areas, educators work to instill in students values that help them be productive, respectful, and respected.

In using the categories above to analyze instructional goals, teachers may find that the goal is primarily content-oriented. A sample adapted from the Virginia Standards of Learning for Earth Science (Commonwealth of Virginia, 1995) is shown in Figure 2.6 (p. 20).

FIGURE 2.6. EARTH SCIENCE: CONTENT-ORIENTED GOAL

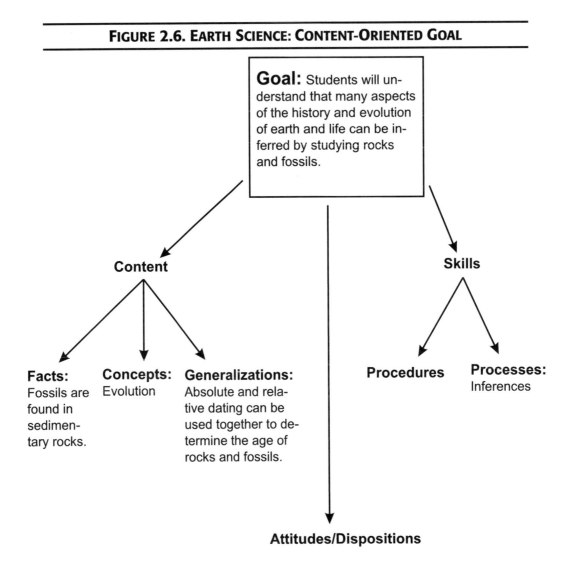

For this Earth Science unit of instruction, the teacher will want to choose teaching and assessment strategies that lend themselves best to remembering facts, understanding concepts, and using inference to reach a generalization. Based on the way the teacher has "unpacked the goal" here, the unit would not appear to include a great deal of direct, hands-on experience or higher-level thinking (except for the process of inference, which may or may not actually be *taught* within this unit). An open-ended essay question or a well-constructed objective test may be the best choice here. Consider, however, the very different focus of the example in Figure 2.7.

FIGURE 2.7. ENGLISH: PERFORMANCE-ORIENTED GOAL

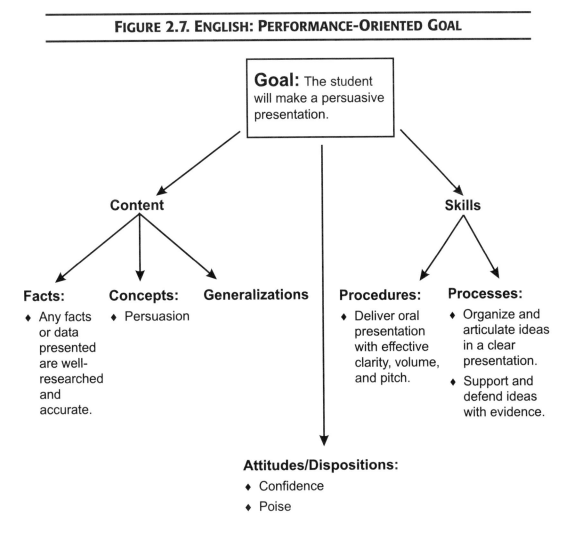

In this example (Figure 2.7), the learning is much more performance- and skill-focused. Therefore, it makes sense to plan an assessment that has the student actually prepare and deliver a persuasive presentation. Lessons and activities in the unit would be geared to providing instruction, guidance, and feedback as the student works toward the performance.

BLOOM'S TAXONOMY OF EDUCATIONAL OBJECTIVES

Like the unpacking chart, Bloom's *Taxonomy of Educational Objectives* (1956) provides a framework for thinking about instruction and assessment, and can be a helpful tool for teachers in connecting the two. In general, the *Taxonomy* acts as a guide for classifying the verbs found in curricular and instructional objectives. Thinking about this language can be a starting point in the critical process of articulating exactly what we are expecting students to learn. When the target is clearly described, then the most effective strategies for instruction and assessment can more easily be developed. For example, if an objective calls for students to define, describe, or identify, then assessments should be developed that gather evidence that students can perform these tasks. Care needs to be taken not to view each verb in isolation, but to examine it within the context of the entire instructional objective.

Figure 2.8 provides examples of the classification of key verbs often used to describe instructional objectives.

FIGURE 2.8. CLASSIFICATION OF KEY VERBS

◆ **Knowledge**

define	identify
name	label
list	recall

◆ **Comprehension**

explain	paraphrase
describe	translate
summarize	give example

◆ **Application**

apply	experiment
solve	demonstrate
show	prepare

◆ **Analysis**

classify	differentiate
compare	infer
contrast	interpret

◆ **Synthesis**

design	develop
create	compose
construct	invent

◆ **Evaluation**

judge	debate
evaluate	assess
criticize	critique

Bloom's *Taxonomy* is often considered as a hierarchy that may be used to order skills from the simple to the more complex. Working within this view, teachers organize the skills from the simple to the complex, building learning just as one would construct a house, from the ground up. Fogarty and Bellanca (1989) speak of "three-story intellects." First-story intellects gather information, second-story intellects process information, and those making it to the third story of intellect apply information.

Building on this approach to the organization of skills, teachers may organize assessments in the same manner, matching controlled-response items with skills that require knowledge, and open-ended performance tasks with skills that require students to think, synthesize or evaluate information. We suggest that the skills be viewed not as a linear model, but rather as a spiral, one that is constantly in motion, with students knowing, applying, and evaluating information simultaneously. In this model, skills are not placed in discrete boxes and presented in a lock-step fashion, but are integrated in classroom instruction and assessment.

The wording of the assessment item or the products or performances required of the students may vary according to the level of cognitive skills required of students. The following two tasks are designed to assess the students' knowledge and understanding of the impact of the Continental Congress on the government. Figure 2.9 is an example of a controlled-response assessment that requires students to provide a limited number of short-answer responses.

FIGURE 2.9. CONTROLLED-RESPONSE ASSESSMENT

List three accomplishments and three failures of the Continental Congress.

Skills Required:

- *Knowledge.* Recall information about the American Revolution and the acts of the Continental Congress.

- *Comprehension.* Understand the authority of the Continental Congress and the climate in which the decisions were made.

- *Application.* Apply knowledge of cause and effect to examine the actions taken by the Continental Congress.

- *Analysis.* Compare and contrast the actions of the Continental Congress in order to distinguish between accomplishments and failures.

Figure 2.10 is an open-ended question (essay) that provides the student with a greater opportunity to be involved in the production of the response. The cognitive skills that are required are similar to those for the previous task, but are extended to encourage a greater level of critical thinking.

FIGURE 2.10. OPEN-ENDED (ESSAY) ASSESSMENT

You are the editor of a newspaper that is sympathetic to the British cause. Write an editorial on the accomplishments and failures of the Continental Congress.

Skills Required:

- *Knowledge.* Recall information about the American Revolution and the acts of the Continental Congress.
- *Comprehension.* Understand the authority of the Continental Congress and the climate in which the decisions were made.
- *Application.* Apply knowledge of cause and effect to examine the actions taken by the Continental Congress.
- *Analysis.* Compare and contrast differing perspectives.
- *Synthesis.* Create an editorial for a given period in time.
- *Evaluation.* Judge the accomplishments and failures of the Continental Congress from a given perspective.

As evidenced by the controlled-response task in Figure 2.9 (p. 23), it should not be assumed that the instruction to "list" requires students to function at the cognitive level of knowledge only. The open-ended assessment task in Figure 2.10 is an example of how a writing task can become an assessment tool that requires students to use a range of cognitive skills from knowledge to evaluation. In both tasks, students must move in and out of the cognitive levels to demonstrate their understanding of the influence of the Continental Congress on the politics, economy and society of the time.

ASSEMBLING AN ASSESSMENT TOOLKIT

Let's say you're about to undertake a home improvement project—one that will require the use of a variety of tools during various phases of the job. You would start by examining the project carefully and making sure of what you want to accomplish (i.e., clarifying the goal). Next, you would be smart to go about *gathering* and *organizing* the variety of tools that you will need to complete the project. To gather the tools, you might first determine what tools you already have, get them out, and be sure that they are in working order. Then, you would plan to acquire those you will need, perhaps by shopping for them, or borrowing from the neighbors! Next, you would get your tools organized, perhaps in compartments of a toolbox. You might sort them by function, arrange them by size, or use some other organization scheme. The important thing is that you have a way of finding or accessing the tool you need at the time you need it, depending on the requirements of the job you are doing.

The design of assessment in a block schedule involves the same sort of process. Questions teachers might ask that have to do with *gathering assessment tools* include:

- ◆ What instructional strategies and assessment techniques will likely be most effective for the content and skills I want students to learn?

- ◆ What strategies and techniques do I already know that I can use?

- ◆ What new strategies or techniques might I need to learn? How, where, and from whom will I learn them?

- ◆ What do I know about my students (their prior knowledge, their learning styles, their previous experience) that might steer me toward or away from a particular approach?

Just as teachers need an expanded repertoire of instructional strategies in order to meet the diverse needs of their students, so, too, they need a range of effective assessment techniques. Standardized measures of student performance serve a purpose in education, but they should not become the only measure of gauging the depth of student learning. A critical eye is needed when examining evaluation instruments. Teachers need to identify the inherent limitations and the opportunities provided by various assessments. The value of any assessment strategy should be measured in terms of its relationship to teaching and learning.

Given the extended periods of time offered by block scheduling, teachers have opportunities to expand their repertoire of effective instructional and assessment strategies, and thus might consider a wider range of assessment ideas than they used in a traditional schedule. With tools such as Bloom's *Taxonomy* and the unpacking chart (Figure 2.5, p. 18) as guides, teachers can focus student assessment directly at the knowledge, skills, and dispositions they want students to learn. For example, in a unit where students will be learning skills and increasing their depth of understanding, assessment might take the form of performance tasks or projects. When the assessment tool is a long-term project, teachers can even structure opportunities for students to receive feedback *during the course of the assessment*. This enables them to reflect on and revise their work, thereby improving performance. Although teachers will always want some student work to be done completely independently (and rightly so!), there is a legitimate place in the assessment process for guidance, feedback, and *learning*.

With many of the time constraints imposed by a traditional six- or seven-period day eliminated, teachers in a block schedule are free to explore these and other assessment methods. They are able to choose from alternatives ranging from the familiar and traditional multiple-choice test to more open-ended models, such as interviews and portfolios. These options are the tools in the teacher's assessment toolkit. It may be helpful to think about this toolkit using the framework shown in Figure 2.11.

FIGURE 2.11. ASSESSMENT TOOLKIT

Controlled-Response Tests	Open-Ended Questions	Performance Tasks
Short answer, fill-in-the-blank	Essays	Oral presentation
True/False	Graphic organizers	Demonstration
Multiple choice	Debate or discussion	Project or exhibition
Matching		

To assess student learning effectively, teachers should use a variety of assessment methods from the toolkit. The decision about which type of assessment to choose depends on what skills and content are being assessed, and where this learning fits in the overall instructional plan for the course. Sometimes the purpose of assessment is to check student understanding of a basic skill that will later be applied as part of a more complex process. For example, a teacher may want to check students' measurement skills before launching a unit where students will be using measurement in a science experiment. In history, the teacher may want to review and give a quiz on the traditions and beliefs of major religions before working with students to analyze the historical impact of religious differences on political and social structures. In instances such as these, a traditional paper-and-pencil test is probably the best assessment choice.

More performance-based, open-ended assessments should be considered when the learning to be assessed consists of essential "big ideas" and thinking or process skills. When students can demonstrate their learning in a real-world context, by actually *using* what they have learned in a product or performance of their own making, the assessment process maximizes and helps "cement" the learning in place. Performance assessments are useful when teachers want to assess depth of conceptual understanding rather than recall of facts; that is, when teachers want to find out what students know and what they can *do* with what they know.

Teachers must be alert to the variety of ways in which they can gather evidence of student learning. Typically, student responses are in the form of written products, as on a short-answer test or essay. In other cases, teachers observe student performance directly, and document it using a checklist, an anecdotal record, or perhaps an audio recording. As we discuss in Chapter 7, a collection of student work can be organized into a portfolio in order to communicate learning over time.

In this chapter, we presented frameworks and suggestions to help teachers organize their planning process so that they are linking curriculum, instruction, and assessment. First, use of the *unpacking chart* (Figure 2.5, p. 18) clarifies our learning goals, identifying exactly what is it that we want students to know and be able to do. Second, Bloom's *Taxonomy* assists us in deciding how students will demonstrate what they have learned. Do we simply want them to recognize the elements on the periodic table, or do we want them to comprehend the characteristics of these elements? Will they be expected to analyze a compound to determine what elements it contains? Third, the *assessment toolkit* (Figure 2.11) guides teachers in choosing the assessment tools that will best demonstrate what students have learned.

Much of this book is devoted to providing teachers with the guidelines, techniques, hints, and examples needed to choose and use a variety of assessments wisely. In the following chapters, we examine each type of assessment tool, with an emphasis on how it might best be used in a block schedule.

3

ONGOING ASSESSMENT THAT PROMOTES STUDENT LEARNING

How often should student learning be assessed? Every day! Most tests and performance assessments occur at the end of instructional units and give the teacher a snapshot of what students have learned during the preceding time period. These "summative assessments" are important, but they should not be a teacher's only assessment information. We believe that effective teachers take advantage of opportunities within their daily classroom activities to gather information about student learning. This process of ongoing assessment can alert teachers—long before the "official" test is given—to misunderstandings or difficulties that students are having. Ongoing assessment, built into the instructional process, enables teachers to give students feedback that helps them to learn and improve *during* the unit. This practice yields greater learning and better performance when the time comes for the end-of-unit test.

When assessment takes place during a unit of instruction, with feedback and opportunities for revision, students learn during the assessment process itself. Weaving informal assessment into a unit improves instruction by showing teachers what students are learning "along the way," so that alternative approaches, re-teaching, extensions, enrichment, and other adjustments can be introduced.

Final assessments (such as a unit test or culminating performance task) can serve to communicate expectations to students. If the assessment will be based on a rubric outlining what the teacher will look for, sharing the rubric early on lets students be clear about these criteria. When the assessment is to be a performance task, the teacher may provide models of student work that *do* and *do not* meet the criteria, so that students can analyze these models and think about how their own work can be improved. In the case of an objective test, such as true/false or multiple choice, the teacher might share and discuss sample questions or provide a study guide that reflects the targets set at the beginning of the instruction. These techniques help students understand what the format of the assessment will be, what the important learning is that they are expected to demonstrate, and what the teacher will be looking for in their responses. This clarity gives students the best possible opportunity to perform well—isn't this what we want? When assessment is unclear, "tricky," or secretive, we have no way of knowing whether the work we are getting from students is their best. Consequently, we lose confidence in the validity of the assessment to document what students really know and can do.

In this chapter, we describe three types of tools for informal classroom assessment. Questioning, visual organizers, and cooperative learning strategies —all excellent *instructional* tools—also can be used effectively for *assessment*.

QUESTIONING: PROBING STUDENTS' THINKING

Questioning is a strategy found in most classrooms. Teachers ask questions to encourage student attentiveness and to check for understanding. In the words of Eggen and Kauchak (1996), "Questioning...helps students maintain sensory focus, provides communication of important concepts through repetition, and is an effective way of informally assessing student understanding" (p. 40). The responses provide the teacher with valuable information regarding what students know—*or don't know.* A wise teacher uses this information to inform instruction. Answers provided by the students can serve as checkpoints for the teacher. If the answers to the questions are correct, the teacher may conclude that there is a general understanding of the information. If the responses indicate confusion and lack of understanding, the teacher should be aware that additional explanations or alternative instructional approaches might be needed.

As Figures 3.1 and 3.2 illustrate, the ways teachers use questions can serve either to end or to extend teacher-student interactions. In Figure 3.1, the teacher asks a question, receives a response, and labels the response as correct or incorrect. At this point, the interaction about this question is over; the teacher moves on to another question or another topic. The student is not invited to explain the response, nor are other students given the chance to react to the response.

FIGURE 3.1. QUESTIONING TO RECEIVE A RESPONSE

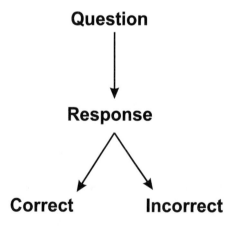

Compare this interaction to that shown in Figure 3.2, where, instead of immediately labeling the response as correct or incorrect, the teacher asks a follow-up question. This invites further thinking, both by the student who gave the response and by other students, who now have opportunities to participate in the discussion. The student finds out whether the student's response is correct or incorrect, but also receives input and additional information. Figure 3.2 shows three ways that this might occur. Building on the student's response to formulate follow-up questions, the teacher may provide corrective feedback, have students clarify their responses, or extend the learning.

FIGURE 3.2. QUESTIONING FOR INCREASED INTERACTION

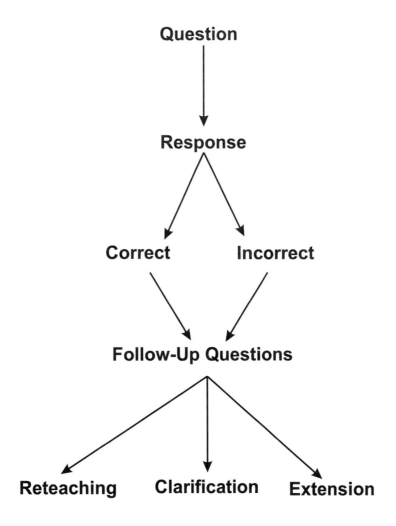

The use of questions to gather assessment information can be likened to the use of landmarks when traveling. Any of us who have traveled past our own front doors know the importance of using signs, checkpoints, or landmarks to guide our way. If we set off on a road that we expect will take us to our final destination, yet become so absorbed in negotiating traffic that we forget to monitor our own progress, we may miss a turn. Too late, we realize that we have spent valuable time traveling in the wrong direction. Many a domestic dispute has arisen because someone *failed to read the signs*! Disregarding the useful information that can be found in student responses is like driving past the road sign—it was there all along, but we passed it by.

The usefulness of the information that can be gained from student responses is directly related to the types of questions asked and to the quality of the questions. Costa (1991) refers to the "awesome power" teachers have "to prompt students to perform cognitive behaviors." According to Costa, this power resides in the teacher's "careful and selective use of questions and statements" (p. 196). Unfortunately, the level of questioning in classrooms is often limited to questions that allow yes/no or right/wrong responses. Fogarty and Bellanca (1989) refer to this type of question as a "skinny" question. Ask a "skinny" question and expect a response of "yes," "no," or "maybe so"—or perhaps a shake of the head, a shrug of the shoulders, or a single-word reply.

This type of questioning merely enables the teacher to ask questions and provide immediate feedback to the students. The "initiation-response-reaction" form of questioning encourages a recitation of knowledge and limits the students' involvement in the dialogue that occurs, as Wilen (1991) points out in his summary of research on questions and questioning:

- Teachers ask questions that primarily require students to recall basic information. Minimal emphasis is placed on encouraging students to think about what they have memorized.

- Higher-cognitive-level questions encourage students to think critically, particularly when students are pushed to clarify, explain, and support their responses.

- Recitation is the primary form of oral interactive discourse in classrooms, as evidenced by teacher use of the initiation-response-reaction pattern and a high frequency of knowledge-level questions.

- Students take little initiative during recitations and discussions and ask few questions. This may be due to the controlling influence the teacher maintains during interactions with students. (pp. 32–33)

Classroom interactions provide opportunities for teachers and students to exchange ideas and opinions. Unfortunately, these "discussions" often are one-sided, with the teacher controlling much of the conversation. Kemp, Morrison, and Ross (1998) include "instructor-directed" discussions as only one of three types that can be planned as part of the instructional process.

- *Instructor-directed.* The exchange of ideas within the group is limited because the flow of the conversation is from the teacher to the student. Questions are posed by the teacher and answered by the students.

- *Group-centered.* This form of discussion allows for a "free-flowing exchange of ideas" among the members of the group. The group controls the questions and the pace of discussion. The flow of the discussion depends upon the interaction among the members of the group.

- *Collaboration.* Problem solving is the basis for this form of discussion. The teacher acts as a resource to the group. Shared decision making is an essential element of this form and participants are "obliged to accept and integrate the ideas presented and critically evaluate the alternative solutions." (p. 154)

Time can be a factor that influences the teacher's decision to use the "instructor-directed" style of questioning. Schedules that limit class periods to 45 minutes do not encourage teachers and students to involve themselves in a deep exploration of content or issues. As class time is limited, so, too, is planning time—time that is needed for teachers to develop questions, to analyze student responses, and to plan for instruction. Teachers working in a traditional setting with 125 or more students may feel overwhelmed by the number of contacts that need to be made with students and may be more interested in the quantity rather than the quality of the questions that are asked.

Block scheduling provides extended periods of time in which teachers can pose questions and present problems that stimulate thinking and encourage students to process information. Rather than feeling the need to rush through a series of questions, teachers may be more inclined to take time to encourage students to think before they respond. The importance of this strategy is evidenced in the following:

> Essential to student thinking, especially at the higher cognitive levels, is the amount of time a teacher allots for student reflection after asking a question and before a student responds, and immediately after the student responds before the teacher or another student reacts. (Wilen, 1991, p. 20)

The work of Rowe (1974) points to the importance of utilizing "wait time" to provide time for students to process the questions and to formulate their responses. In her studies, it was found that with increased "wait time" came an increase in the length of student responses and in the number of questions students asked. As students are encouraged to think before they react, a signal is sent that students are expected to be active participants in the learning process, thinking and processing information rather than sitting, receiving, and reciting.

Time alone is not enough to stimulate students to process information. One question can encourage students to expand their thinking; another can limit and control the responses. Of course, we recognize that asking a "good" question does not guarantee that complex, thoughtful responses will be elicited from students automatically. As Newmann (1991) points out, "Merely presenting students with higher order challenges will not necessarily help them to develop the competence to meet the challenges successfully." The knowledge of subject matter, the skill to apply the information to "new problems" and an attitude or disposition of "thoughtfulness" must be combined if students are to respond to questions and challenges that require them to be critical thinkers and problem solvers (pp. 324–340). When students have difficulty providing quality answers to such of questions, the teacher has the opportunity to assess in which area the difficulty lies. Follow-up or probing questions may reveal whether the student is missing content knowledge, lacks application skills, or is not interested or not willing to persist in the completion of a complex task.

The importance of developing thoughtful problem solvers is pointed out in the National Council of Teachers of Mathematics Standards (NCTM, 1989). For students to learn to "communicate mathematically," they must have opportunities to communicate their ideas, clarify their thinking, and refine and consolidate their thoughts. Asking students to explain their answers encourages thinking rather than guessing. It places a responsibility upon the students to organize their thoughts and to be prepared to justify their thinking.

Students who are unaccustomed to this expectation are often caught off-guard when asked a follow-up question. See what happens when a student gives a correct answer to a question and you follow with an immediate, "Tell me why you responded this way." More often than not, the student will hesitate and then proceed to change his or her answer! As teachers, we tend to use the traditional smile, nod, or positive affirmation to indicate that a student has responded correctly. The "tell me why" request most often is reserved for the student who responds incorrectly; in probing the student's thinking, we hope to unravel the unclear thoughts and misunderstandings.

However, if we reserve the follow-up "why" for incorrect responses, we limit our ability to encourage *all* students to be reflective. In effect, we cut short the thought process by stopping the dialogue and moving on to the next question or activity. We recommend asking questions such as those in Figure 3.3 as prompts to encourage students to elaborate on their thinking.

One challenge of using questioning strategies effectively is to involve *all* the students in the process. If patterns of response become fixed and students begin to see that the eager hand-wavers will always be called upon, their attentiveness diminishes. An element of expectation must be maintained in order for students to focus on the questions and to pay attention to the responses of their peers. Gall and Rhody (1987), Morgan and Saxton (1991), and Wilen (1991) offer suggestions for involving students. We included many of their suggestions with our own in Figure 3.4 (p. 39) to provide tips for involving students in the interactions of questions and answers. These tips are focused on raising the attention level of all students, thus communicating the expectation that they will listen, think, and respond.

VISUAL ORGANIZERS:
SEEING WHAT STUDENTS ARE THINKING

To monitor student thinking and to check for understanding, it helps to have a variety of strategies that will engage all students. One method for determining whether students understand information is to provide opportunities for them to organize the information. A common method of organization is the outline. Students learn to develop a linear plan for writing, for analyzing an author's work, or for arranging the steps of a procedure. Students may understand the process of outlining and still have difficulty organizing the information. This may be because they see the learning as discrete bits of information and fail to see connections, or because they do not understand the information well enough to organize it in a meaningful way. The students' inability to organize information can alert the teacher that students need additional support in order to process the information effectively.

The use of visual organizers provides opportunities for students to expand their organizational skills from a linear approach to one that is more holistic. Hyerle (1996) refers to visual organizers as "tools" for learning. Seen as such, visual organizers provide students with frameworks for organizing their thinking—and provide teachers the opportunity to *see* how students are thinking. Hyerle's experiences with "webs" illustrate the assessment benefits associated with the use of organizers:

> Students could externalize and safely show their interrelated thinking patterns; I could see what was once internal, invisible, inaccessible. I finally could view what *and* how each student was thinking about the content I taught—I also discovered certain problems. Students' maps often revealed a storm of clouded concepts. But these clouds were a point of learning, an opportunity. I could access and assess my students' misconceptions and their confusion about how to further organize, prioritize, delete, and clarify the overwhelming amount of associated ideas they had drawn. (p. 2)

Visual organizers range from the simple to the complex. They may be used as part of the instructional process to present concepts, to outline procedures, or to compare and contrast events. Perhaps the most well-known visual organizer is the Venn diagram. The interlocking circles are used to compare information, particularly to display similarities and differences. Other organizers, such as webs, position information according to categories and subcategories, arranging them from the global to the specific. Yet another group of organizers demonstrates the linkage of events in a sequence or cycle. Teachers who incorporate the use of organizers into their instruction enhance opportunities for student learning by providing visual representations of information.

(Text continues on page 40.)

FIGURE 3.3. TELL ME WHY

Asking follow-up questions encourages students to reflect and to justify their answers. Try using these follow-ups to stimulate thinking. Be ready to examine the students' answers to learn more about how they are thinking and responding to instruction.

♦ Why did you respond this way?

♦ How did you come up with this answer?

♦ Explain your thinking that led you to this answer.

♦ Describe the process you used to reach this conclusion.

♦ Show me the steps that you took to solve the problem. Explain them as you go along.

♦ Outline the procedure you used to come up with your response.

♦ Can you defend your answer? Why or why not?

♦ Is this problem like any you have solved before? How does it compare?

♦ What would happen if…?

♦ If you had to solve a similar problem, would you use the same method? Why or why not?

Encourage students to take a stand and to express confidence in their answers. If they are unable to do this, then this should be a signal that they are uncertain about their knowledge of information and their abilities to *use* the information. Remember the importance of providing a classroom atmosphere that supports students and encourages them to take risks. Responses will be limited if students feel threatened.

**FIGURE 3.4. QUESTIONS AND ANSWERS:
TIPS TO INVOLVE STUDENTS IN THE PROCESS**

♦ Ask the question of the class as a whole, rather than directing the question to a particular student. Provide time for students to think about the answer before calling on someone.

♦ To encourage students to listen to the response of others, ask follow-up questions that require students to paraphrase what another student has said or to add to the response of the first student.

♦ Jot it down. Ask a question and then give students a few moments to "jot down" an answer before calling on someone.

♦ Occasionally ask a question that requires a group response, such as "Raise your hand if you think...."

♦ Practice "wait time." Give students ample time to think and to respond. Three to five seconds has been recommended as the optimal wait time (Rowe, 1974).

♦ Ask probing questions that encourage students to explain their responses.

♦ Ask one question at a time. Be careful not to string questions together. Provide sufficient time for students to think about a question and respond to the question before asking another one.

♦ Provide feedback that is specific rather than general. "Good answer" does little to help the students learn *why* this was an appropriate response.

♦ Use the Think-Pair-Share strategy. Ask a question; allow time for students to think of a response; and then pair the students and have them share their responses with their partners.

♦ Call on students randomly. Place the name of each student on a note card. Keep the cards handy, using them as a deck from which to draw. Pose a question or a problem, wait for everyone to think of a response, and then select a card from the deck and call on that student. Be sure to maintain the attention of the students by returning the card to the deck after each question is answered.

Once students become familiar with the organizers and have practiced using them, the teacher may find the organizers to be useful tools for assessing students. As a teacher moves about the room monitoring the students' use of an organizer, it is easy to see which students are struggling with the organization of the information. Missing information is apparent, not lost in the wordiness of long, written explanations. As teachers watch students use and create organizers, they have opportunities to get instant snapshots of the students' thinking.

Visual organizers may be used to introduce material, as a model for review, or as part of the assessment process. The examples that follow (Figures 3.5 through 3.9, pp. 41–45) are models for teachers to use as they develop their own organizers.

For additional ideas on visual organizers, we suggest these resources:

- *The Cooperative Think Tank: Graphic Organizers to Teach Thinking in the Cooperative Classroom* by James Bellanca.

- *Visual Tools* by David Hyerle.

- *Creating Success in the Classroom! Visual Organizers and How to Use Them* by Patty Tarquin and Sharon Walker.

- *Inspiration* (software) available from Inspiration Software, Inc. at www.inspiration.com

COOPERATIVE LEARNING: OBSERVING STUDENTS AT WORK

Teachers working in schools with extended classroom periods are exploring a variety of models of instruction. Included in these models is cooperative learning. Block scheduling provides extended periods for cooperative teams to work together to accomplish group goals. As teachers monitor the work of the groups, they have the chance to observe and record student behaviors. As students discuss issues, explain their thinking, and review information, teachers have opportunities for informal assessment of the students' learning. Cooperative learning activities can range from those designed for review of skills to others that require students to discuss issues, develop hypotheses and reach conclusions.

Cooperative activities can be designed to require students to interact in many different ways in order to accomplish a group goal. The activities by John Strebe shown in Figures 3.10 (p. 45) and 3.11 (p. 46) involve students in solving problems and discussing and defending their solutions. The "1-2-4 Activity Plan" and the "Team Discussion and Circle of Knowledge" are described by Strebe in the book, *Teaching in the Block* (Canady and Rettig, 1996).

(Text continues on page 46.)

FIGURE 3.5. COMPARE-AND-CONTRAST ORGANIZERS

Organizers may be used to help students see similarities and differences. When students analyze information and present the results using an organizer, they present a picture of their thoughts on a single page. The Venn diagram is commonly used to provide a visual display of comparisons. Teachers and students who find the size and shape of the Venn to be limiting should explore other models of organization, such as those pictured below.

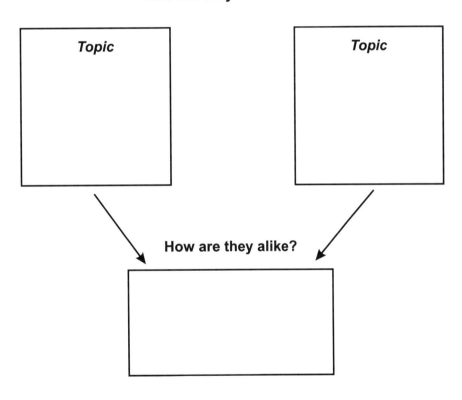

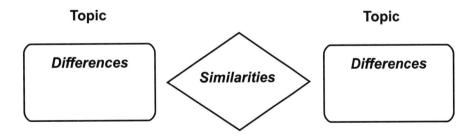

FIGURE 3.6. TOPICS FOR COMPARE-AND-CONTRAST ORGANIZERS

Ask students to compare and contrast:

♦ Rock types (igneous, sedimentary and metamorphic)

♦ Renewable and nonrenewable resources

♦ Physical and chemical changes

♦ The Earth's atmosphere to that of other planets

♦ The developmental stages of different organisms

♦ Plane figures

♦ Quadrilaterals (parallelogram, rectangle, square, rhombus, and trapezoid)

♦ Points of view

♦ Facts and opinions in newspaper reports

♦ Authors' styles

♦ A speaker's verbal and nonverbal messages

♦ The advantages and disadvantages of storage and retrieval technologies

♦ The elements of character, setting, and plot in one-act plays

♦ National, state, and local government

♦ Theological differences between major religions of the world

♦ Civilizations

♦ Monarchies

♦ Political platforms

♦ Major wars

♦ Political and economic systems of countries

♦ Current health issues and health issues from a selected period of history

---

FIGURE 3.7. THE WEB

The web consists of a group of shapes and lines that are organized according to categories. The size and the positioning of the shapes are used to indicate relationships. A central idea forms the basis for the development of this organizer.

Students can use a concept map to prepare for writing, to organize notes or to prepare for oral presentations. At a glance, the students' thinking about the topic can be seen.

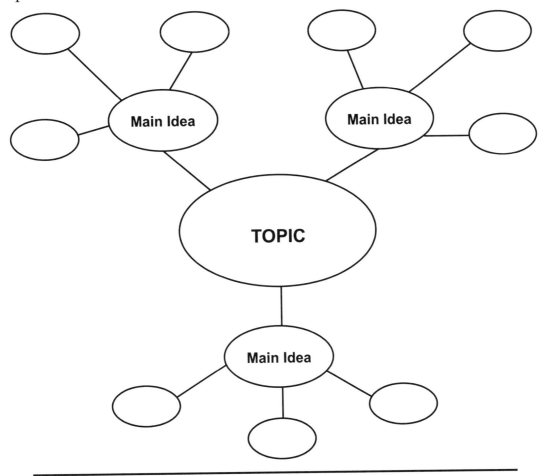

Tarquin and Walker (1997) suggest that students consider the following questions when they use organizers as a prewriting activity:

- What is my topic?
- What are some things (main ideas) about my topic I want to talk about?
- What details, reasons, examples, or explanations can I give to each main idea so my reader really understands what I am writing about? (p. 86)

FIGURE 3.8. SEQUENCE AND CYCLE ORGANIZERS

There are certain procedures, processes or events that occur, have occurred, or need to occur in a particular order. Organizers may be used to emphasize a step-by-step process, so that each step is defined clearly yet seen as a part of the total process. Looking at a sequential organizer, it is easy to see the number of steps in the process and to determine whether the process is linear or cyclical. The following two organizers are examples of the types of models that can be developed to display a sequence or cycle of events.

Sequence of Events

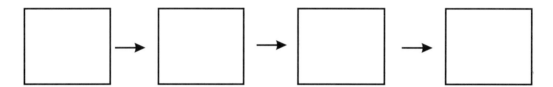

Cycle of Events

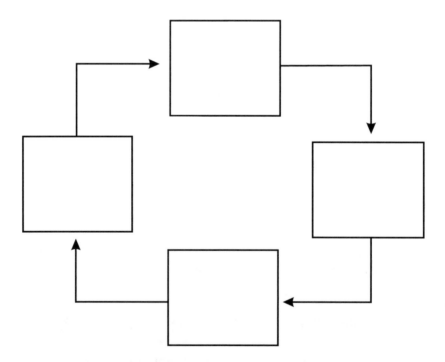

FIGURE 3.9. TOPICS FOR SEQUENCE AND CYCLE ORGANIZERS

♦ Sequences
  • Process by which a bill becomes a law
  • Steps in factoring a polynomial
  • Events in a period of history
  • Steps in the scientific process
  • Procedure for creating a spreadsheet
  • Steps in dissecting a frog
  • Procedures for safe food handling

♦ Cycles
  • Stages of the life cycle of a butterfly
  • The water cycle
  • Cyclical themes in literature
  • Population cycles
  • Historical cycles of events

FIGURE 3.10. 1–2–4 ACTIVITY PLAN

---

1. Students are given a worksheet.

2. Each student is instructed to complete the assignment individually.

3. After an appropriate length of time, students are allowed to pair with a teammate to discuss their work, achieving consensus in some cases and disagreeing in others.

4. Teams of four are formed and a discussion leader is appointed.

5. Teams reach final conclusions on answers.

6. Class sharing is conducted.

SOURCE: Strebe, John (1996). "The Collaborative Classroom," in R.L. Canady and M. D. Rettig, *Teaching in the Block*. Larchmont, NY: Eye on Education. Used with permission.

FIGURE 3.11. TEAM DISCUSSION AND CIRCLE OF KNOWLEDGE

1. Students are given a question or problem.

2. Time is provided for students to think, write, and work individually without interruption until each has determined a response.

3. A team leader is appointed for each cooperative team.

4. The team leader conducts a group discussion of the question. The group considers the contributions of each person and examines the defense of different conclusions.

5. After considering the contribution of each team member, the team reaches consensus.

6. A "circle of knowledge" is conducted in which each team leader gives his or her team's conclusion and, where appropriate, the team's defense.

SOURCE: Strebe, John (1996). "The Collaborative Classroom," in R.L. Canady and M. D. Rettig, *Teaching in the Block*. Larchmont, NY: Eye on Education. Used with permission.

Activities such as "Focused Discussions" (Johnson, Holubec, & Johnson, 1988) help students focus on the topic of study and summarize their understandings. Another activity, "Academic Controversies" (Johnson, Johnson, & Holubec, 1994) challenges students to work cooperatively to examine and discuss controversial issues. We suggest that you consider the following resources if you are interested in learning more about using cooperative strategies in your classroom:

♦ *Teaching Foreign Language in the Block* by Deborah Blaz.

♦ *Teaching in the Block* by Canady and Rettig.

♦ *Enhancing Thinking Through Cooperative Learning* by Davidson and Worsham.

♦ *Cooperative Learning in the Classroom* by Johnson, Johnson, and Holubec.

♦ *Creative Controversy: Intellectual Challenge in the Classroom* by Johnson and Johnson.

♦ *Cooperative Learning* by Spencer Kagan.

No matter what the assignment, students need to know what is expected of them, both individually and as a group. Johnson, Johnson, and Holubec (1988) suggest that lesson guidelines be established and communicated to students. To support the effectiveness of the cooperative group, these four areas need to be addressed:

- *Academic Task—The Group Goal:* State what students are to do: answer the questions, design a model, and so on.

- *Criteria for Success:* State how the successful completion of the task will be determined.

- *Positive Interdependence:* Discuss how each member of the group will support the learning of others.

- *Expected Behaviors:* Specify the appropriate behaviors for students working on the cooperative task. Identify behaviors that will be monitored and evaluated.

It is helpful to develop a list of expected behaviors, such as listening, asking questions, or the like, that can be charted and monitored. Also useful are anecdotal records that include student interactions, comments, and questions. Charting this information on a form, such as the one provided in Figure 3.13 (p. 49), enables the teacher to monitor the process of the group as well as assess the performance of individuals within the group. Remember to be as specific as possible when describing expected behaviors. For example, it may be necessary to describe the characteristics of active listening or discuss what it means to offer constructive criticism. One activity that may help students develop cooperative skills is to identify characteristics of effective interactions on a T Chart, like that shown in Figure 3.12 on page 48.

FIGURE 3.12. A T CHART

COOPERATION

What does it look like?	What does it sound like?

ACTIVE LISTENING

What does it look like?	What does it sound like?

FIGURE 3.13. COOPERATIVE LEARNING ACTIVITY

Observation Form

Cooperative Group Name/Number_____

Group Members

1:

2:

3:

4:

Group Goal_____

Date(s)_____

Students

Skills	#1	#2	#3	#4
Listens without interrupting				
Asks questions				
Contributes to group discussion				
Offers support and encouragement to group members				
Remains on task				

NOTES:

Analyzing the cooperative learning experience should not be the sole responsibility of the teacher. Team members should be trained to reflect upon the experience "in order to discover what helped and what hindered them in completing the day's work and whether specific behaviors had a positive or negative effect" on the team (Johnson, Holubec, and Johnson, 1988). There should be time at the end of a cooperative activity for students to discuss their performance and to compare their behaviors with established criteria for effective cooperative interactions. Feedback from the observer can stimulate discussion and reflection. Groups can use the results of these discussions to plan methods of improvement.

A primary benefit of cooperative learning activities is that students have the opportunity to support each other as they strive to learn facts and examine issues. An essential element of cooperative structures is interdependence. As students work together to achieve a common goal, they begin to see the benefits of working with others. Once this level of trust is developed, the possibilities for students to work together as *partners in learning* are increased.

As students develop skills, practice methods and procedures, and apply what they have learned, they need feedback focused on specific performance criteria. Once these criteria are established, students can use them as guides to assess their learning and that of their peers. Teachers who share the responsibility of assessment with their students remove the mystery that often shrouds the process and help students see the connections between performance and assessment. Involving students in assessing themselves and their peers also increases the opportunities for students to receive feedback.

When students have a clear understanding of expectations, they can serve as assessment partners to other students, providing feedback and opportunities for discussion of products and performances. Students can conduct peer reviews of writing, listen to and offer feedback for students rehearsing musical instruments, and check procedures such as those used in scientific investigations. The students who are working as partners can apply the same criteria the teacher will use to assess student learning. Checklists or rubrics provide specific "look fors" that can guide observations, evaluations, and discussions.

We suggest that teachers explore methods such as those outlined in Figure 3.14 for involving students in cooperative partnerships. As students work together, teachers can monitor their interactions and provide individual help as needed.

In this chapter, we discussed and illustrated three of the many strategies teachers might use to assess student learning on a day-to-day basis. A teacher who is interested in obtaining quality feedback realizes that assessment of student learning is embedded in the instructional process. It is a *part* of the lesson, rather than the final event that signals the lesson is over.

FIGURE 3.14. IDEAS FOR PARTNERS

♦ Share your written works with a partner. Read and discuss.

♦ Practice for a debate. Present arguments and have partner react as the opposition might.

♦ Speak before an audience. Rehearse a speech with a partner.

♦ Develop a mathematical problem. Exchange problems with a partner. Solve the problem and exchange again to check the answers.

♦ Work with a partner to perform a scientific experiment. As partners, check to make sure all procedures are followed and documented.

♦ Practice using your foreign language skills with a partner. Practice asking and answering questions.

♦ Discuss with a partner the sequence of events that lead to a particular moment in history. Have your partner check your accuracy.

♦ Play a musical selection that you are memorizing. Have your partner read the music to follow you as you play.

♦ Create a piece of art that communicates a certain emotion. Share your creation with a partner. Ask your partner to identify the emotion that the art evokes.

♦ Work with a partner to graph an equation. One person sketches the graph by hand; the second partner creates the graph using a graphing calculator. Then compare graphs to see if they match.

4

CONTROLLED-
RESPONSE TESTS

Historically, the controlled-response test format has been the assessment choice for teachers, textbook publishers and designers of standardized tests. Although the primary form of this type of testing is the ubiquitous multiple-choice test, other forms include true/false, matching, and fill-in-the-blank. Objectivity and ease of scoring are seen as two of the benefits of this type of testing. The fast pace of instruction in a traditional schedule has forced many teachers to choose test formats that are easy to administer and score. Faced with more than 100 students a day, teachers who want to provide timely feedback to students have created tests that can be scored quickly with the use of an answer key or scanned through a scoring machine.

Controlled-response tests have several benefits. For example, they are

♦ Efficient to administer in groups;

♦ Easy to score;

♦ A straightforward way to assess content knowledge;

♦ Useful in the middle of a unit to check for understanding; and

♦ A way to practice for high-stakes accountability tests.

Controlled-response tests generally are used to measure "knowledge, not skill" (Haladyna, 1994). The measurement of knowledge does not imply that the tests are made up of simplistic questions that require a regurgitation of facts. Well-designed test items should cause students to think. According to Haladyna (1994), "Multiple-choice test items are generally regarded by testing specialists to be more difficult to prepare than essay items" (p. 24). Time and thoughtful consideration are needed to design quality test items. The answers to multiple-choice and true/false tests should not be so obvious that no thought is required. On the other hand, the "multiple-guess" approach to test design should be avoided.

Three students were heard discussing a test they had just completed. When asked how she did on the test, one student responded, "I either got an A or an F. I don't have any idea how I did." The other students seemed to agree that their scores might also range from one end of the grading spectrum to the other. The reason for the confusion and frustration became evident when one young man stated, "That was the trickiest test I ever took." How many times have you felt this same frustration? The "gotcha" approach to testing forces students to spend time and energy figuring out the "trick" of the test writer, rather than focusing on the information to be learned. Such tests serve to accentuate what the students do not know, rather than to identify what the students do know. Students who are consistently exposed to this type of testing see no connection between what they know and how they perform. Limited feedback (in the form of a grade or a few "red-inked" comments) provides little or no incentive for students to improve.

Stiggins (1997) believes that well-written test items "frame challenges" for students that allow for the selection of best answers. Tests should be aligned so closely to instruction that students see the connections between the questions they are being asked and the instructional activities in which they have been involved. Students who see connections between what they do in class and what they are asked to complete on a test are more likely to become interested in demonstrating their knowledge than those who see no relation between the two.

A factor that encourages the use of controlled-response tests is the increased emphasis on standardized tests as a measure of student achievement. It cannot be denied that students faced with standardized tests need experience taking tests designed in a multiple-choice format. These tests serve as an important part of the assessment process. However, they should not become an end to the instructional process, but a means of informing instruction. Given extended periods of time in the block schedule, teachers now can move beyond the use of controlled-response items simply to test the recall of information, extending these items to encourage students to expand their thinking and to apply the information. In addition to increasing the depth of their questions and tasks, teachers working in block schedules have time to review test questions, have students explain their answers, and correct misinformation.

Controlled-response tests can have disadvantages, as well. Because of the nature of questions having a single correct answer, these tests rarely provide opportunities for students to improve performance after the first try. Feedback to students may be in the form of a numerical score or letter grade only, although many teachers provide qualitative feedback to help students learn. Controlled-response tests, such as true/false and short-answer formats, make it difficult to assess a skill directly; the student can answer questions about the skill, but not perform it. For example, a student may be able to correctly match foreign language vocabulary words to their meanings, but may be unable to pronounce the words or use them in a conversation.

Frameworks such as those presented in Chapter 2 can assist teachers in capitalizing on the strengths of controlled-response tests, while minimizing their drawbacks. Remember that the goal is to choose assessment techniques that measure learning effectively and reflect classroom instruction.

Controlled-response items *can* be designed to assess learning at a variety of cognitive levels. Controlled-response tests, such as the widely used multiple-choice format, often are characterized as assessing only low-level cognitive skills, such as recall. It's true that the simple remembering of information is probably best assessed with these types of test items. However, properly designed controlled-response tests also can assess students' ability to apply and think critically about what they know.

Figure 4.1 (p. 58) provides basic tips for teachers to consider when developing controlled-response tests. The list is compiled from the work of Guskey (1997) and Popham (1999). For further explanation of the items and for additional information on test design, we suggest you consult the books *Implementing Mastery Learning* by Thomas T. Guskey and *Classroom Assessment: What Teachers Need to Know* by James Popham.

EXTENDING CONTROLLED-RESPONSE QUESTIONS

One limitation of the controlled-response test format is the lack of opportunity for students to explain their thinking or to apply the information they know. Even within the range of controlled-response items, presenting the question in different ways can increase the level of difficulty for the students. The three examples in Figures 4.2 (p. 59) assess the same knowledge. However, notice that in the first example the answers are provided; the student need only select the correct one. In the second example, students must supply the list themselves. In the third example, students must not only generate the list, but they must also show how they would use the vocabulary in a sentence.

(Text continues on page 60.)

FIGURE 4.1 TIPS FOR CREATING CONTROLLED-RESPONSE TESTS

- **Two-Choice Items (true/false, right/wrong, fact/opinion, accurate/ inaccurate, etc.)**
  - Avoid items that are blatantly true or false, right or wrong.
  - Focus on one concept or significant idea in each item.
  - Avoid using double negatives.
  - Avoid terms such as always, never, usually, and sometimes.

- **Matching**
  - Develop homogeneous lists so that all responses are likely selections.
  - Provide more responses than premises. This prevents students from selecting the final answer by using the process of elimination.
  - Select matching items that are brief. Place the shortest items to the right.
  - Clearly state guidelines for matching, including whether or not items maybe used more than once.

- **Multiple Choice**
  - Construct the stem so that it contains a clearly stated question or problem.
  - State the stem in positive rather than negative form.
  - Develop incorrect alternatives that are plausible and that require students to analyze the choices.
  - Design alternative responses that are consistent in length.
  - Vary the position of the correct response.
  - Avoid "all of the above" alternatives and use "none of the above" with caution.

- **Completion (short-answer questions, problems, or incomplete sentences)**
  - Structure the item so that a single, concise response is needed.
  - For incomplete sentences, make all blanks equal in length.
  - Avoid clues to the answer, such as the use of *a* or *an*.

FIGURE 4.2 PRESENTING THE QUESTION: THREE EXAMPLES

Example 1

Match the Spanish and English words for these foods.

Corn	A. manzana
Onion	B. pepino
Potato	C. uvas
Apple	D. cebolla
Grapes	E. pina
Pineapple	F. papa
	G. maiz

Example 2

List six fruits and vegetables. Provide the English and the Spanish name for each.

Example 3

While vacationing in Mexico, you stop by a local supermarket (supermercado) to buy a few groceries (comestibles). Write your grocery list in English and Spanish.

Be prepared—just in case you cannot locate one of your items, write a question that you could ask someone who could help you find what you need. Write your question in English and in Spanish.

STRATEGIES FOR REVIEWING BASIC KNOWLEDGE, FACTS, AND PROCEDURES

Beginning at an early age and continuing throughout adulthood, we encounter basic facts, bits of information and procedures that serve as a foundation of knowledge on which we build understandings. From the recognition of numerals to the identification of the elements in the periodic table, we establish methods for remembering. Most of us remember clever mnemonics presented by our teachers that help us recall lessons from our past. (Just hear someone say "ROY G BIV" and we automatically begin to think in Technicolor—red, orange, yellow, green, blue, indigo, violet.) The assessment of basic facts or knowledge of procedures may often take the form of a controlled-response test. Rather than just presenting the information to students and leaving it up to them to develop memorization techniques, however, teachers need to take the time to help students develop strategies for learning. Opportunities for students to rehearse, elaborate, and organize information increase the likelihood that when the test day arrives, what was taught will have been learned and remembered. Weinstein and Mayer (1986) examine the teaching-learning process and point to the need to integrate the "product" and "process" goals of learning to enable students to process information.

> …[T]here are two different kinds of activities that influence the encoding process: (1) teaching strategies, such as the teacher presenting certain material at a certain time in a certain way; and (2) learning strategies, such as the learner actively organizing or elaborating or predicting about the presented material (p. 316).

The extended periods of time in a block schedule offer opportunities for teachers to help students process the information that has been presented and develop strategies for learning.

Figure 4.3 is a list of suggested activities that will involve students in the process of learning. Monitoring the students as they work allows an informal assessment of how well they understand the information.

MOVING BEYOND THE TEST AS AN END

Too often, tests are seen as an *end* to the instructional process, rather than as part of the process. Too often, tests at the conclusion of a unit of study signal to students that a cycle of learning is ending; only after the tests does another cycle begin. Too often, tests are taken, graded, and returned with little discussion of the learning that *did* or *did not* take place. Block scheduling, however, provides time for teachers to involve students in the evaluation process, even when traditional controlled-response tests are given. Rather than handing papers back with a grade and no comments, teachers can take the time to review the test items with students. When discussing the tests, teachers should encourage students to explain why they selected their answers, both the correct and the incorrect. Guskey (1997) suggests using a

FIGURE 4.3 ACTIVITIES FOR REVIEW

♦ *Pause to Ponder.* Take time to pause during a presentation, the viewing of a video, or the reading of textbook information to ask students to reflect on what they have seen or heard. Give them a few minutes to record major points or questions they have. Involve the group in a discussion of their "ponderings."

♦ *The Ideal Method* (Bransford and Stein, 1984). Use the IDEAL method of problem solving to help students develop their problem-solving skills.

  • *I*dentify the problem.

  • *D*efine the problem.

  • *E*xplore possible strategies for solving the problem.

  • *A*ct on the identified strategies.

  • *L*ook at the effects of your efforts.

♦ *Picture This.* Provide time for students to create visual images to represent vocabulary words or concepts that have been presented. (For more information on using visual images in the classroom, see Nancy Margulies' *Mapping Inner Space*.)

♦ *Tell a Story.* After studying a famous person, learning about a historical event, or solving a problem, have the students take on the role of storytellers. Students work individually or in small groups to create a story that summarizes the information they have learned.

♦ *Focus Trios* (Johnson and Johnson, 1988). Prior to a film, lecture, or reading, form trios of students and have them work together to summarize what they already know about the subject and develop questions that they have about it. Following the presentation or reading, the students answer their questions, discuss new information, and develop new questions.

♦ *Organize It.* Teach students a variety of methods to help them sort, classify, and organize information. Guide students in the identification of main ideas and supporting details. *Model* the use of outlines, webs, and graphic organizers before encouraging students to create their own.

♦ *Write a Question.* After material has been studied, have students write a question that would measure someone's understanding of the material. Record each question on an index card. Select questions to be used as a daily review of the material.

double answer sheet, such as the one found in Figure 4.4, to provide immediate feedback to students. Students responding to test items record their answers twice, once on the "student" side of the paper and again on the "teacher" side. When they are finished with the test, they tear the answer sheet in half, keep one side, and turn in the other side to the teacher. As soon as all papers are turned in, the teacher reviews the test questions and the answers, and students can check whether their answers are correct. The teacher can then evaluate the students' original responses and return them at the next class meeting.

Another method of involving students in the assessment process is presented by Conti-D'Antonio, Bertrando, and Eisenberger (1998) in *Supporting Students with Learning Needs in the Block*. The authors outline a strategy to involve students in test preparation from the day the material is introduced in class. The method shown in Figure 4.5 (p. 64) provides a process that involves students in the prediction of test items. The students' questions and the identified rationale are "used for rehearsal and retrieval and practice and as part of a debriefing process after the test" (p. 125).

The reteaching of information should be built into the cycle of instruction and assessment. This can be accomplished by teachers on a continuing basis within class periods, or can be built into a schoolwide schedule. One example, the 75–15–75–15 plan (see Canady and Rettig, 1995), sets aside blocks of time at the end of each term for remediation, enrichment, and community service. This plan is shown in Figure 4.6 on page 65.

Opportunities for students to learn from their mistakes should be a natural part of the classroom environment. The expectation that students *will* learn means that teachers must recognize that students do not all learn at the same pace, and must provide opportunities for continuous progress toward the course objectives. One way to do this is to provide opportunities for students to retake tests. This may range from students studying and retaking the test items that they missed, to completing alternative assignments, to taking a different form of the original test once they have had more time to study. Simply reviewing the content may not increase the student's knowledge or skills; tutoring or other forms of reteaching may be necessary. It's essential to outline clear procedures for the retaking of tests, leaving no room for misinterpretation, and to establish firm timelines and guidelines for completion of the work. Rules for grading should be understood by all.

Despite their limitations, controlled-response test items can be an effective means of assessing student learning. We suggest that teachers take care to design items that are valid measures of what students know; misleading or "trick" questions should be avoided. We also recommend that teachers adapt and adjust traditional controlled-response questions in ways that make them more interesting and challenging for learners.

FIGURE 4.4 DOUBLE ANSWER SHEET

Answer Sheet	
Name _____	Name _____
Date _____	Date _____
DIRECTIONS: Circle the letter of the correct answer or write the answer on the blank beside the number.	DIRECTIONS: Circle the letter of the correct answer or write the answer on the blank beside the number.
1. a b c d e _____	1. a b c d e _____
2. a b c d e _____	2. a b c d e _____
3. a b c d e _____	3. a b c d e _____
4. a b c d e _____	4. a b c d e _____
5. a b c d e _____	5. a b c d e _____
6. a b c d e _____	6. a b c d e _____
7. a b c d e _____	7. a b c d e _____
8. a b c d e _____	8. a b c d e _____
9. a b c d e _____	9. a b c d e _____
10. a b c d e _____	10. a b c d e _____

SOURCE: Guskey, T.R. (1997): *Implementing Mastery Learning,* 2nd ed. Belmont, CA: Wadsworth, p. 101. Reprinted with permission.

NOTE: This format could be used for two-choice items, such as true/false or fact and opinion (a or b); for matching items with up to five options (a to e); for multiple-choice items; and for single-word completion items.

FIGURE 4.5 PREDICTING TEST QUESTIONS

Steps

1. Label a section of a notebook *Test Questions*. Divide the page into three columns—main idea (answer), critical information (question), and rationale (why you picked the ideas and information).

2. After each lecture, reading assignment, classroom activity, or homework assignment, add questions to your list. Record at least two for each main idea.

3. Confirm the information with a study partner or the instructor.

Test Questions for the Battles of the Civil War		
Important Topic	*Critical Information*	*Rationale*
Lincoln	1. Who made a speech after the Battle of Gettysburg? 2.	Mr. C. said it three times today.
Antietam	1. What is the most famous Civil War battle fought in Maryland? 2.	Book and Mr. C. talked about this.
Sherman	1. Which Union general ordered the burning of Atlanta? 2.	End of chapter questions and notes.

4. Use the list as a structure to help you study for the test.

5. After taking the test, compare your list with the test to see if your information was complete.

SOURCE: Conti-D'Antonio, M., Bertrando, R., and Eisenberger J. (1998). *Supporting Students with Learning Needs in the Block*. Larchmont, NY: Eye On Education. Used with permission.

FIGURE 4.6 THE 75–15–75–15 PLAN

	Fall Term *75 Days*	*Middle Term* *15 Days*	*Spring Term* *75 Days*	*End Term* *15 Days*
Block I *Periods 1 & 2* *112 minutes*	Science	Enrichment, Elective, Community Service, Remedial Work, etc.	English	Enrichment, Elective, Community Service, Remedial Work, etc.
Block II *Periods 3 & 4* *112 minutes*	Health/ Physical Education		Art	
Period 5/L *48 minutes + 24 minutes for lunch*	Band and Lunch	Band and Lunch	Band and Lunch	Band and Lunch
Block III *Periods 6 & 7* *112 minutes*	Math	Enrichment, Elective, Community Service, Remedial Work, etc.	Social Science	Enrichment, Elective, Community Service, Remedial Work, etc.

SOURCE: Canady, R.L., and Rettig, M.D. (1995). *Block Scheduling: A Catalyst for Change in High Schools.* Larchmont, NY: Eye On Education. Used with permission.

5

OPEN-ENDED
"ESSAY" QUESTIONS

In the past, teachers have relied upon controlled-response tests partly because they are efficient to administer and score. Teachers striving to assess a range of student learning opt for assessments that can be completed in a class period. In traditional schedules, this may limit their choices to controlled-response formats. Block schedules create opportunities for teachers to employ a greater range of assessment strategies, including essay questions. These questions probe deeply into students' thinking about the content they have learned.

Open-ended or "essay" items require students to construct their own responses to questions in situations where the teacher is assessing particular thinking and processing skills and/or deep understanding of content. In this chapter, we refer to "open-ended" and "essay" items interchangeably. Other kinds of assessments, such as portfolios and performance tasks, are open-ended in nature but are not necessarily written essays. We address these types of assessments in subsequent chapters. Here, we are discussing only written responses to teacher-designed questions. These questions require more lengthy responses than short-answer questions, and often are designed to assess students' thinking and reasoning skills as well as their understanding of content.

BENEFITS OF OPEN-ENDED QUESTIONS

Open-ended questions require students to generate their own responses rather than simply selecting a correct response from a list of choices. This approach has major advantages for the teacher who wants to find out not only what students know, but also how they are thinking. First, students can't get the correct answer by guessing. In the previous chapter, we discussed methods for extending controlled-response formats in ways that require students to go beyond simple recall of information. Even so, students are selecting from a limited number of possible answers. The student who brings little or no knowledge to the assessment may pick the correct answer by chance.

Second, what about students who have a great deal of information to share? In typical "objective test" formats, these students can communicate only a limited range of knowledge. Open-ended questions enable these students to go beyond the "expected" answer to provide a more sophisticated, in-depth, or creative response. Therefore, teachers not only know which students meet expectations and which don't, but they also know which students exceed expectations on the assessment.

Using open-ended questions, teachers have the opportunity to assess both content knowledge and thinking skills at the same time. Open-ended items generally call for students to *use*, rather then simply *remember*, what they have learned. An open-ended item is a good assessment choice when the teacher wants students to use knowledge in ways like those shown in Figure 5.1.

FIGURE 5.1. IDEAS FOR FRAMING OPEN-ENDED QUESTIONS

- Apply knowledge by using it in a new situation or connecting it to previously learned material.

- Compare and contrast compositions.

- Predict patterns in history.

- Apply mathematical properties in new problems.

- Use thinking skills to generalize, synthesize, or create.

- Develop a theory based on observations and/or research.

- Solve a problem in more than one way.

- Design an experiment to answer a question.

- Integrate science content with current social issues.

- Use thinking skills to examine content and issues deeply and analytically.

- Analyze a literature selection.

- Examine an issue from a different perspective.

- Justify an opinion or point of view.

- Explain a phenomenon.

- Interpret a work of art.

Marzano and Kendall (1996) use the following example to illustrate how an essay question on the Lincoln-Douglas debate requires students to use specific reasoning skills:

> Douglas and Lincoln said many things in their debate. Identify their areas of agreement as well as their areas of disagreement. Then select one of their areas of disagreement and analyze the arguments each has presented to determine which one has presented the best case. In your analysis, look at the logic of each argument as well as the accuracy of their information. (p. 115)

As Marzano and Kendall point out, this prompt reveals how well students know the issues debated and the positions taken by Lincoln and Douglas. It also requires students to use their knowledge to "identify similarities and differences" and "analyze an argument"—both important skills for students of history.

Even in a field such as mathematics, where essay questions are infrequent, teachers should recognize that open-ended questions can be effective assessment tools. The Mathematical Framework for the 1996 National Assessment of Educational Progress (1996) recommends the use of open-ended questions to assess "mathematical power":

> It is here that the NCTM recommendation that students experience a number of extended open-ended items requiring construction of responses is important. Through a student's report of his or her own thinking, the questions of the relevance of an approach, nature of reasoning, and ability to solve problems becomes less of a high-inference guess and more a conclusion that can be drawn from evidence. (p. 38)

DESIGNING OPEN-ENDED QUESTIONS

Open-ended questions can be tough to design, especially for teachers who want to assess challenging goals such as those above. Simply jotting down a broad, vague question that "covers all the bases" won't get the quality assessment information that teachers need. To design open-ended questions that can serve as effective assessments, teachers must know the characteristics of excellent questions. Key features of quality essay questions are listed in Figure 5.2. We will elaborate on and illustrate each of these key features.

FIGURE 5.2. KEY FEATURES OF QUALITY ESSAY QUESTIONS

A good open-ended question:

♦ Is based on clear criteria

♦ Is specific

♦ Is valid

♦ Is interesting and challenging

♦ Reflects instruction

A GOOD ESSAY QUESTION
IS BASED ON CLEAR CRITERIA

First, designing open-ended questions requires teachers to articulate clearly the learning goals that are to be measured. If the question is to measure depth of understanding, then the teacher must know and communicate to students what kinds of responses would indicate this depth. If the question is intended to measure thinking skills, then both teacher and students must be clear about what those skills are and what aspects of a response "count" as acceptable evidence of the skills. Clear expectations help students focus their responses on the most salient content and skills while allowing for a variety of right answers (i.e., answers that meet the criteria).

Assume, for example, that the teacher has identified *comparing and contrasting* as an important skill. Ask any ten teachers to grade a student's response to a "compare and contrast" essay question, and chances are they won't agree on the score. Why? Because these ten teachers do not share a common definition of the skill. Suppose, however, that we provide those ten teachers with the following list of criteria that define the skill.

When students *compare and contrast*, they should:

♦ Note similarities and differences. This means more than just listing traits of each item. There should be a real explanation of ways in which the items are alike and different.

♦ Develop a thorough comparison that is clearly related to the context of the question or problem.

♦ Use an organization tool such as an outline or a Venn diagram to prepare a response.

♦ Draw conclusions or generalizations based on the comparison, giving some reasonable interpretation.

Now our fictional ten teachers know what to look for in the student's response, and chances are good their scores will be more consistent.

When teachers begin a unit of instruction by articulating the learning goals and their associated criteria, they create clear *targets* toward which students can direct their thinking and effort. This reduces confusion and misperceptions in students' minds, and increases the extent to which they can focus and be productive. It assures students that they know "what the teacher is looking for" and takes the guesswork out of learning.

After criteria are established and communicated (and *taught*, of course), they become the basis for the design of open-ended questions. By sticking to the criteria, teachers know that their questions are assessing what they intended to assess, and students know what the question will be asking them to do. The question, while remaining open-ended in nature, should be closely aligned to the criteria and specific enough so that students who demonstrate the criteria will meet the expectations for a quality response.

A GOOD ESSAY QUESTION IS SPECIFIC, BUT IT ALLOWS FOR A VARIETY OF ACCEPTABLE RESPONSES

Essay questions that are very general or vague seldom give teachers meaningful information about what students have learned. Students who have *not* met the instructional goals can respond with a broad, weak, but acceptable answer. Those who know quite a bit about the content may write lengthy responses that are full of accurate information, but stray from what the teacher intended. Well-designed questions provide direction for students by reflecting the criteria for success.

Open-ended questions that are vague may be more a test of students' ability to read the teacher's mind than a test of what they have learned. A well-designed question may be difficult for students to answer, but a poorly designed question can leave students wondering what the response should be about! Remember that the reason we give tests is to find out what students know and can do; our purpose is *to get a clear and accurate picture of student performance.*

Teachers may worry that by making an essay question *too* specific, they are giving away the answer. In the design process, teachers may find that in order for the question to have sufficient structure, they essentially must outline the one and only correct answer. If this is the case, then it is likely that an open-ended question isn't the best assessment tool to choose. Rather, this content may lend itself better to a selected-response or short-answer format.

The challenge for teachers, then, is to create questions that are sufficiently clear, but open-ended enough to allow for various responses. The following examples (see Figures 5.3, p. 74; 5.4, p. 74; and 5.5, p. 75) show three versions of the same essay prompt. These examples demonstrate that a prompt *can* be open-ended without being vague, and that it can be specific while still encouraging students to think for themselves.

In an art unit entitled "Surrealistic and Fantastic Art," students are presented with the task shown in Figure 5.3 (adapted with permission from Sue Oliveri, teacher in Albemarle County, Virginia).

FIGURE 5.3. OPEN-ENDED PROMPT

Assess and interpret *Persistence of Memory* by Salvador Dali. Give a critical response to the work as design, and discuss the relationship between the piece and the culture in which it was created.

This prompt likely will solicit a variety of responses from students. Certainly, one purpose of an open-ended prompt is to allow students to respond with a variety of ideas. However, the question must give sufficient guidelines so that student responses that are "on target" can easily be distinguished from those that are "way off." To accomplish this, teachers often provide students with guidelines for structuring their answers. By adding a focusing statement to the question above, the teacher has provided this additional structure (see Figure 5.4).

FIGURE 5.4. PROMPT WITH FOCUSING STATEMENT

Assess and interpret *Persistence of Memory* by Salvador Dali. Give a critical response to the work as design, and discuss the relationship between the piece and the culture in which it was created. *Be sure that your answer includes the elements of the art critique process we discussed in class.*

It is clear now that the question assesses not only knowledge about this particular piece of art, but also the extent to which students remember and understand some predetermined "elements of the art critique process." Those who don't know these elements will not meet the criteria for a quality response, no matter how much they may ramble on about *Persistence of Memory.*

As an alternative, suppose the teacher wants to assess students' ability to respond to each of the elements, but doesn't see *memorizing the elements* as essential. In this case, the teacher might provide focusing questions that students could use to structure their answersas shown in Figure 5.5.

FIGURE 5.5. PROMPT WITH FOCUSING QUESTIONS

Assess and interpret *Persistence of Memory* by Salvador Dali. Give a critical response to the work as design, and discuss the relationship between the piece and the culture in which it was created. Be sure your answer includes the following elements of the art critique process:

- **Description**—What do you see? (Observe carefully and notice detail.)

- **Analysis**—How is the work organized? (Think about how this artist uses the elements and principles of design in this piece.)

- **Interpretation**—What is the artist saying? (Your interpretation can be based on feelings, but these feelings must be supported by what you actually see in the artwork and by your knowledge of the time and culture in which it was created.)

- **Judgment**—What is the artistic merit of this work? (Give your opinion supported by solid reasoning.)

The prompt is still open-ended enough to solicit students' best performance, but now it is targeted specifically toward the important criteria so that the students can concentrate their efforts on what matters most. It is important for teachers designing open-ended items to recognize that students have a right to know the teacher's expectations. Making expectations clear is not cheating—it's *teaching!*

A GOOD ESSAY QUESTION IS VALID

As a student, did you ever try "bluffing" your way through a response to an essay question? Maybe you thought that if you covered lots of lines and pages, the teacher would overlook the fact that you didn't really have much to say. Perhaps you kept your response very general, with lots of repetition and few examples. From an assessment point of view, a very revealing question is: "If you *did* bluff, did it *work*?"

Some essay questions don't discriminate as well as they should between students who understand the content and those who don't. The issue of validity is one that teachers must consider in order to be confident that the question is really assessing the targeted knowledge and skills. The question must be framed so that only those students who can meet the criteria can respond successfully to the question.

Consider, for example, the essay question, "What do you think was the most significant invention of the twentieth century? Tell why." A student, especially one who is a good writer, could respond to this question with very little knowledge of twentieth-century technological advances, which is the content the teacher intended to assess. Compare this question to the following essay prompt: "Choose an invention from the twentieth century. Identify the inventor. Describe the specific technological advances that led to this invention, and where these technologies are found within the invention." The added specificity and focus in this prompt require the student to recall and apply major concepts from the unit.

The validity of essay questions is also at risk when teachers deduct points for aspects of the student's response such as handwriting, formatting, neatness, or spelling. Although these skills are important and might well be graded separately, using them as a measure of content knowledge invalidates the question.

A GOOD ESSAY QUESTION ENGAGES STUDENTS BY BEING INTERESTING AND CHALLENGING

Writing open-ended questions that are interesting to students is important for several reasons. First, students are more likely to try harder and do their best when the question interests them. Second, when they are engaged in an interesting task, students are more likely to persevere long enough to compose a complete and detailed answer. In short, interesting questions get better responses, and better responses mean increased student performance on the assessment.

Consider the two examples of questions covering the same content shown in Figures 5.6 and 5.7.

FIGURE 5.6. OPEN-ENDED QUESTIONS: EXAMPLE 1

Consider the formula $F = 10(S - 55) + 40$.

♦ In your own words, describe what this formula means.

♦ Solve for F if $S = 74$, showing the steps you use.

♦ Solve for S if $F = 250$, showing the steps you use.

♦ If F has a range from 90 to 340, what is the range of S? How did you find this?

♦ Compare the formula above to the formula $F = 3(S - 55) + 29$. For a given value of S, which formula yields the lower value of F?

FIGURE 5.7. OPEN-ENDED QUESTIONS: EXAMPLE 2

The fine for speeding on the highways in most states is a function of the speed of the car. In Connecticut, the speeding fine can be determined by the formula:

$$F = 10(S - 55) + 40$$

♦ In your own words, describe what this formula means.

♦ What would your speeding fine be if you were driving at 74 miles per hour? (Show or explain how you found this.)

♦ Suppose you received a speeding ticket for $250. How fast were you going? Show the steps you used to arrive at your answers, and the reason for each step.

♦ The minimum speeding fine in Connecticut is $90. The maximum speeding fine is $340. What is the range of speeds that corresponds to these fines? (Show or explain how you found this.)

♦ The speeding fine in Virginia is $F = 3(S - 55) + 29$. If you were driving too fast, in which state would you rather get a ticket? Why?

SOURCE: Used with permission from Steve Leinwand,
Connecticut Department of Education.

The examples in Figures 5.6 and 5.7 illustrate a simple premise: essay questions are more engaging if they have a *context*. The designer of this math question has chosen the context of speeding tickets and fines—one that appeals to students who may be new drivers or anticipating being able to drive—in order to give the question some degree of purpose. That is, the question is *about* something that students find inherently interesting.

Another way to provide context for an essay question is to *personalize* the question. If the students see that the question has something to do with *them*—even indirectly—they are more likely to engage with the question and produce a quality response. Not all the content that we want students to know has direct application in their lives at the time they learn it. Still, some questions can be personalized by creating a simulated role for the student, as in example 3 in Figure 5.8.

FIGURE 5.8. OPEN-ENDED QUESTIONS: EXAMPLE 3

The life circumstances of men and women are as much the ingredients of history as are laws and treaties. Your assignment is to write an auto-biographical sketch of yourself in one of the roles listed below (your choice).

♦ You are Jessie Grady, a 40-year-old female factory worker during World War II.

♦ You are Karl Johanny, a 26-year-old German-American living in a Midwestern city and working in a steel mill during World War I.

♦ You are David Emery, a 35-year-old worker in the Civilian Conservation Corps during the Depression.

An acceptable response must describe the nature and character of your occupation and role, and place it as carefully and as fully as possible in historical context. Include information about your economic circumstances, your hopes and fears, your relationships with family, friends, and coworkers, and your perspectives on the major issues of the day.

SOURCE: Adapted with permission from Scovie Martin and Jamie Brown, teachers in Albemarle County, Virginia

Students also tend to be interested in questions that allow room for their own creative thinking. One way to assess content and still encourage creativity is by asking content-based "what if" questions. To answer these questions well, students must have a solid understanding of the content. They then build on this understanding while predicting, generalizing, and even speculating about a hypothetical situation. The situation may be realistic, somewhat realistic, or downright fantastic. A few examples of "what if" questions are shown in Figure 5.9. Note that these questions are *not* very specific. However, any of them can be accompanied by a short description of essential elements of a quality response, as in the history question above.

FIGURE 5.9 "WHAT IF" QUESTIONS

♦ What if there were no ozone layer above the earth?

♦ What if all people were millionaires?

♦ What if everyone drove electric cars?

♦ What if there were no laws governing traffic?

♦ What if dinosaurs were reintroduced through genetic engineering?

♦ What if Shakespeare had written rock and roll?

♦ What if income taxes were eliminated?

♦ What if the atomic bomb had not been dropped?

♦ What if only those with money could buy voting rights?

♦ What if everyone in the world spoke the same language?

♦ What if Thomas Jefferson could be president today?

♦ What if *pi* equaled 5?

♦ What if the manual to your VCR were written as a poem?

♦ What if Picasso had painted the Mona Lisa?

♦ What if forest fires were eliminated completely?

Another way for teachers to personalize questions is to ask students to present and justify their own reasoned opinions about issues being studied. We all know that adolescents and teenagers *have* opinions about issues, and they're willing—sometimes more willing than we'd like—to share them! Middle and high school students are learning to connect their own ideas and values to issues in the larger community and society. They enjoy and readily engage in debate, discussion, and (as parents can attest) argument. With some teaching and feedback, students can learn to provide reasoning for their positions on issues, and to use events and examples to substantiate their arguments. Essay questions that allow students to discuss what an issue means to them, how they perceive it, and why, are engaging for most students. For example, consider this question:

Several health risks have been associated with smoking, both for the smoker as well as for other citizens. What are these health risks and their consequences?

Using this same content, the teacher can ask a question that solicits the student's own opinion and puts the question in a social/political context:

Given what you know about smoking, do you believe that smoking should be banned in restaurants and other public places? Provide a solid rationale for your opinion, which takes into account issues on both sides of this debate.

A GOOD ESSAY QUESTION REFLECTS INSTRUCTIONAL PRACTICE

Thinking carefully about instructional methods is critical to choosing the right kind of assessment for any unit of study. Suppose that a history unit is built around activities in which students read and analyze primary sources, write essays or letters from a participant's point of view, and role play important historical events. Daily, the teacher is guiding students not just to remember, but also to build understanding of events, and to connect these events to both their causes and their consequences. Perhaps students are even comparing this period in history to their own time. These types of instructional activities match up well with open-ended assessment questions that ask students to integrate content knowledge and thinking skills.

Imagine a mathematics class in which students write almost daily. They keep math journals, in which they respond to classroom demonstrations, assess their own progress, and describe their approaches to problem solving. In homework assignments and cooperative learning activities, they discuss which strategies work best for various problems and why. An essay question is a good fit with what goes on in this classroom every day.

In another math class across the hall, students focus on memorizing formulae, "plugging in" numbers, and getting accurate answers. There is little discussion, virtually no attention to higher-level thinking, and most written work is in the form of step-by-step procedures that are demonstrated by the teacher and then replicated in "practice sets" by the students. An open-ended question that asked these students to apply, hypothesize, or generalize would be completely inconsistent with instruction; it would be assessing skills that were never taught.

SCORING STUDENT RESPONSES TO OPEN-ENDED QUESTIONS

To some teachers, a perceived disadvantage of open-ended questions is that they are "subjective" or difficult to score reliably. In contrast, we have found that careful, thoughtful scoring procedures applied to essay responses can be as accurate as (and in some cases, *more* accurate than) scoring of short-answer tests. There are two commonly used approaches to scoring student responses to open-ended items. The first is holistic scoring. This method is used in situations in which the response will be given one score or grade, and the teacher will look at how the student integrates various aspects of the response into a cohesive whole. The second method is analytic scoring. Here, the teacher is looking for certain components or features of the response, each of which receives a separate score or a number of points.

Earlier in this chapter, we discussed the importance of articulating *criteria* that describe the features or components of a quality student response. Using these criteria as a starting point, teachers design either holistic or analytic scoring guides (also called rubrics) that describe the kinds of student responses that would receive each score or rating on a particular scale. The scale might consist of traditional letter grades or might have levels from 1 to 4 or 1 to 5. Some scoring guides (most commonly holistic ones) attach a descriptor to each level of the scale, as in the example in Figure 5.10.

FIGURE 5.10. A HOLISTIC SCORING GUIDE TEMPLATE

Distinguished response—this response exceeds expectations.	*Characteristics of a distinguished response are described here.*
Proficient response—this response meets expectations.	*Characteristics of a proficient response are described here.*
Partial response—this response has some features of a proficient response, but does not meet expectations.	*Characteristics of a partial response are described here.*
Unacceptable response—this response has few or none of the features of a proficient response.	*Characteristics of an unacceptable response are described here.*

The template in Figure 5.10 shows a possible format for a holistic scoring guide with four levels of performance. Regardless of whether the scoring guide is holistic or analytic, and no matter how many performance levels it has, it must contain the criteria for success that were shared with students early on in the unit. In Figure 5.10, the criteria would be reflected in the characteristics of a proficient response.

As an illustration, suppose that students are learning to write persuasively in English class and are studying government in social studies. Persuasive writing criteria for this unit are shown in Figure 5.11.

FIGURE 5.11. PERSUASIVE WRITING CRITERIA

♦ Writing is targeted to a specific audience.

♦ Author's voice is evident.

♦ Persuasive techniques are used.

♦ Conventions of language and mechanics are used.

♦ Writing is organized; message is clear.

In the government class, there will be additional criteria specific to the unit being studied (on current presidential candidates), as shown in Figure 5.12.

FIGURE 5.12. EXAMPLE OF ADDITIONAL UNIT-SPECIFIC CRITERIA

Students should be able to:

♦ Summarize the positions of each of the major candidates.

♦ Synthesize the positions of each of the major candidates (determine how consistent the positions are with one's own beliefs).

♦ Summarize the rationale for each candidate's views on selected issues.

♦ Interpret the candidates' views as they might be perceived by various segments of the population.

An open-ended question to assess both the writing and government question could be designed by the two teachers collaboratively, as shown in Figure 5.13.

FIGURE 5.13. EXAMPLE OF A COLLABORATIVELY DESIGNED OPEN-ENDED QUESTION

Consider the five major election issues we've discussed in class. Based on the positions of each of the three major presidential candidates, determine which candidate you would support. Assume that you were hired by your candidate's campaign to write a speech that he will deliver at our school. You were selected because you strongly support this candidate, and because you know the population of our school well enough to understand which issues students are most interested in and what arguments they will find persuasive. Write the speech.

Using the criteria listed in Figures 5.11 and 5.12, either a holistic or an analytic scoring guide could be developed for rating the students' written speeches. A holistic guide for this question would combine the government and writing criteria into one score, as shown in Figure 5.14 (p. 84).

FIGURE 5.14. HOLISTIC SCORING
GUIDE FOR CANDIDATE'S SPEECH

Distinguished Response	All the indicators for a proficient response are demonstrated, and this writer goes beyond them with a speech that is especially creative or engaging.
Proficient Response	• Effective use of conventions and voice make the speech easy to follow and engaging. • Message is persuasive and demonstrates techniques targeted at a high school audience. • Content of the speech demonstrates understanding of the selected candidate's positions. • Rationale or arguments for the candidate's positions and ways they differ from the positions of his opponents are presented.
Partial Response	Some of the indicators for a proficient response are present, but this speech falls short in one or two areas. May be well written but unpersuasive, because • Persuasive techniques are not used effectively, • Speech is not targeted to the specific audience, or • Positions are not clearly understood, articulated, or argued by the writer.
Unacceptable Response	The speech meets only one or none of the indicators for a proficient response.

Using the same criteria, the two teachers might develop an analytic scoring guide, such as the one shown in Figure 5.15.

**FIGURE 5.15. ANALYTIC SCORING
GUIDE FOR CANDIDATE'S SPEECH**

Indicators	*Score:* 3 = above expectations 2 = meets expectations 1 = below expectations
Effective use of conventions and voice make the speech easy to follow and engaging.	
Message is persuasive and demonstrates techniques targeted at a high school audience.	
Content of the speech demonstrates understanding of the selected candidate's positions.	
Rationale or arguments for the candidate's positions and ways they differ from the positions of his opponents are presented.	

It is important to point out that there are no "right" and "wrong" scoring guides. The guides above represent one possible interpretation of the criteria. These interpretations will vary from teacher to teacher, just as instructional methods and assessment techniques do. Regardless of their content, however, all scoring guides *should:*

♦ Be written in clear language that students will understand.

♦ Be closely tied to the criteria, so that the scoring guide measures the learning it is supposed to measure.

♦ Be shared in advance with students, so they know what the expectations are ahead of time.

♦ Be a fair representation of expected student performance. (Teachers often develop the levels of their scoring guides using work samples from previous students as "anchors" or samples of each level.)

♦ Be unbiased, so that all students have an equal opportunity to meet the standards.

♦ Be valid for the question, so that the indicators on the scoring guide could reasonably be expected to appear in a solid student response.

Scoring guides help teachers to rate student responses accurately and fairly. Just as importantly, they are also valuable instructional tools. We suggest that teachers give students their scoring guides early in any units in which they will be used. As students participate in the sequence of instructional activities leading to each unit assessment, they can check the scoring guide to help them focus on the most important skills and concepts they are expected to learn.

No matter what assessment technique is used, teachers must always be vigilant about validity and reliability. We have addressed validity issues by recommending that teachers examine and reexamine the match between their stated criteria, their scoring guides, and their open-ended prompts and questions. The purpose of this examination is to assure that the question and the scoring guide do in fact measure the learning that is described in the criteria.

Reliability becomes a concern when teachers begin using their rubrics to rate, grade, or score student responses. Reliability is essentially an issue of fairness; we want to ensure that student work is being scored consistently and without bias. There are many ways teachers can increase the reliability of their scoring and maintain high reliability over time.

We recommend that any teacher using a scoring guide involve other teachers in using the same guide, and then compare results. This activity is especially powerful in settings where the teachers who work with the same students (such as the government and English teachers in the example above) score the same papers and compare their interpretations. The process is also quite valuable when applied among teachers of the same content area. For example, science teachers for ninth, tenth, eleventh, and twelfth grades could score a sample of student projects and compare their ratings. This could lead to a more coherent program, with obvious benefits to students.

Two or more teachers should first read the same student response and score it using the selected scoring guide. Next, they should discuss both *how* they rated the response and *why* they rated it as they did. Teachers engaged in this activity sometimes assume that if they all give the paper the same score that there is no need for discussion. We have found, however, that teachers occasionally assign identical scores for very different reasons! So, whether the scores given are the same or different, the discussion that follows is invaluable. As teachers continue to read responses and exchange ideas, they often discover ways to "tighten up" the criteria or the scoring guide. As they discuss their interpretations of various student responses, they talk about the ways in which their interpretations vary. Then, this variability can be examined, negotiated, and reduced, thereby increasing reliability in scoring among teachers who will be using the same or similar scoring guides.

A second activity to maximize reliability is for the same teacher to score the same student paper at different times. Teachers often wonder whether they would give a student response the same score if they had read it when they were less tired, or if it had been in the middle of the pile instead of on top, or if they had read it just after reading an excellent response. To gain insight into questions such as these, we encourage teachers to record student scores on a separate sheet of paper and then to reread a sample of student responses to see if the second score is the same as the first. This can be as easy as selecting three or four papers out of a class set and inserting them randomly back into the pile after they've been scored the first time. Another way to do this, especially if the papers will be read and scored over a period of several days, is to reread one or two of the same papers each day. A paper that closely parallels the "proficient" or "meets expectations" level of the scoring guide might be selected for this purpose. This student response is one that clearly and solidly meets the criteria, but could not really be described as exceeding those criteria. This paper can serve as an "anchor" for the teacher in the scoring process.

Open-ended essay items are indispensable in a teacher's assessment toolkit, especially in courses where deep understanding of content and ability to apply thinking skills are important. Though they are challenging to design and score, open-ended questions provide teachers with valuable insights into students' thinking. These questions also benefit students, who, in articulating their thinking and describing their understandings, solidify and extend their own learning.

6

PERFORMANCE
ASSESSMENT

Like open-ended questions, performance assessments require students to go beyond the simple recall of information. When teachers choose essay questions as assessment tools, they are asking that students express their responses in writing. Although performance assessments often have a written component, at their heart is the actual "doing" of whatever skills are being assessed. This *performance* might be observed and scored by the teacher as it is occurring, as in these examples:

- Oral presentation
- Musical performance
- Design of a computer spreadsheet
- Dramatic interpretation of an event in history

The teacher could observe these performances in "real time" as the student is doing them, and they would not necessarily require the student to turn in a written product. Other performance tasks, such as a science experiment or a research project, would include a written component.

In the world outside the classroom, people demonstrate what they know and can do in a variety of ways and through a host of media every day. Performance assessments open many of these same options to students, so that they can "show what they know" through a range of tasks, methods, and media.

USING PERFORMANCE ASSESSMENT TO ENGAGE STUDENTS

In the Coalition of Essential Schools, complex performances called exhibitions are used as culminating activities in various courses. These are long-term projects that students work over time to prepare, and that assess the essential learnings from the course. As Ted Sizer (1992) writes in *Horace's School*, "Exhibitions can be powerful incentives for students. Knowing where the destination is always helps in getting there, and if that destination is cast in an interesting way, one is more likely to care about reaching it" (p. 26).

One aspect of exhibitions and other performance assessments that helps engage students is authenticity. Much has been written about "authentic" assessment. The more authentic an assessment task is, the more closely it approximates the way a similar task might be done in a "real-world" setting outside of school. Being authentic means being real, and having a purpose that is more natural than contrived. It stands to reason that when students have opportunities to engage in real, purposeful activity, they will find it more meaningful and motivating than artificial, manufactured activity.

Why, then, have we not *always* done assessment this way? Part of the answer lies in the history and evolution of testing practice, but another important part is related to time. A six- or seven-period day simply doesn't provide the extended time that is necessary for students to be involved in complex, authentic activities. Teachers in all kinds of schools with all kinds of schedules are increasingly interested in performance assessment. Many are finding it successful; many are becoming experts. We assert, however, that teachers in block-scheduled schools have the best possible opportunity to implement performance assessment effectively.

In settings where ample time is available, teachers can worry less about what kinds of activities will fit into a class period. To a greater extent, they are free to imagine the most engaging, interactive, authentic activities through which students could build and demonstrate their skills. When students begin to see that their classroom experiences, *even their assessments*, are interesting and meaningful, they involve themselves more fully and thereby learn more and perform better.

Imagine the way students approach most traditional tests. They may be exhausted from all-night memorization exercises, stressed by the pressure to succeed on a task they've never seen, or resigned to failure before they begin. These students walk into their classrooms on "test days" with a variety of outlooks and attitudes, but it's safe to say that few of them are looking forward to a fun, interesting, and challenging class period.

By contrast, think about the times you've been with students as they made last-minute preparations for a performance. Perhaps it was the baseball team just before the season opener, the cast of the school play at dress rehearsal, or the debate team about to meet their rivals on the stage. These examples represent a different scenario with entirely different feelings and behaviors than those we see on most test days. Students in these settings *are* preparing to be tested, but in ways that are meaningful to them. They have worked to be ready, with coaching from an expert. There will be a real audience, there will be interaction with other students, and there will be feedback on the performance even while it is in progress.

Performance assessment has the potential to be meaningful to students in these same ways. When they know they are learning in preparation for an authentic performance rather than just to take a test and get a grade, students become motivated to do their best. With a greater stake in their own success, they are willing to invest more effort in building the skills they need to succeed.

Designing and Scoring Performance Assessments

In Chapter 2, we discussed the process of planning for and aligning curriculum, instruction, and assessment. We emphasized that, although this process is in theory a set of sequential steps, few teachers apply it in a linear way. Instead, it is integrated and its elements are woven together. Here, we discuss the components of performance assessments and provide advice for designing each component. Again, we must point out that teachers who design performance assessment rarely do it in a predetermined sequence, and rarely do they do it one step at a time. The components must be aligned with and support each other; therefore, the design process calls teachers to revisit each component as new ones are added, adjusting and revising and improving each time. The four components to be discussed in this chapter are listed in Figure 6.1, along with the question that is addressed by each component.

FIGURE 6.1. COMPONENTS OF PERFORMANCE ASSESSMENTS

Component	*Question to Be Addressed*
Goal	What skills and content knowledge will students demonstrate?
Criteria	What characteristics of quality in the students' work will we accept as evidence of their learning?
Rubric	How will the students' work be scored or graded?
Task	What activity or project will the students undertake to demonstrate their learning?

COMPONENT 1: THE GOAL—WHAT SKILLS AND CONTENT KNOWLEDGE WILL STUDENTS DEMONSTRATE?

As we discussed in Chapter 2, teachers must select assessment tools that fit the learning goals being assessed. Because most teachers expect students to learn a range of content and skills, a similar range of assessment types will be needed. Performance assessment is a powerful way to assess student learning and promote student learning at the same time. However, it is not the most appropriate assessment choice in all situations. To use performance assessment effectively, teachers must first examine the learning goals they are working toward, and determine which of those goals lend themselves best to performance tasks.

We recommend that teachers beginning to use performance assessment do so sparingly at first, and begin with the most broad, complex, important instructional goals. Just selecting these goals is challenging—there are so many things that are essential for students to learn. Herman, Aschbacher, and Winters (1992) suggest that we begin by asking:

> What major fields of knowledge, skills, and dispositions are worth teaching and worth assessing? What outcomes are you trying to achieve? Because performance assessments require considerable time and energy—both yours and your students—you will want to focus on a relatively small number of important outcomes, each perhaps representing a month or a quarter's worth of instruction. These assessments should aim at your major learning objectives for students. (p. 24)

Often we ask teachers to identify three or four major skills or understandings that form the basis or structure of their courses. Another way of asking this question is, "If you had to boil your entire course down to its most important learning goals, what would you *insist* that students must know before leaving your class?" In response to this question, most teachers can name a few major skills—for example, reading and interpreting primary sources, designing an experiment, or finding a strategy to solve an unfamiliar problem.

> ...[W]hen an assessment asks a student to conduct a hands-on experiment to determine the optimal environment for a silk worm, we probably are not so much interested in whether the student can identify a healthy environment for silk worms; instead we probably want to use the student performance on this specific task as an indicator of whether he or she can use the scientific method to solve problems. We intend and expect the test to represent something more than the specific object included on the assessment. (Herman, Aschbacher, and Winters, 1992, p. 103)

Although "performance" implies that students are demonstrating their skills, they should not be doing so in the absence of content. That is, students' depth of understanding of concepts and generalizations is evidenced in their application of skills. When choosing content for performance assessment, teachers will want to select the most important or essential components of their courses. Wiggins and McTighe (1998, p. 15) refer to these as "enduring understandings" and contrast them with content that is "important" or "worth being familiar with." In analyzing what they teach and what they want students to learn, teachers often find that many of their instructional objectives are really prerequisites or components that are being used to construct essential skills and understandings. Figure 6.2 lists examples of the types of objectives teachers might teach and assess along the way toward more broad, complex, essential skills.

FIGURE 6.2. EXAMPLES OF TYPES OF OBJECTIVES

Prerequisites or Components	*Essential Skills and Understandings*
Isolate a variable by adding or subtracting a term.	Solve many types of equations.
Identify the parts of speech.	Write to communicate a message.
Describe campaign funding and spending.	Understand the workings of the American political system.
Define Avogadro's principle.	Understand chemical reactions.
Distinguish between fact and opinion.	Defend a position with a logical argument.
Formulate a hypothesis.	Design an investigation to solve a problem or answer a question.
Make a graph of a linear equation.	Organize and display data.
Type text using a computer keyboard.	Communicate through application software.

Examples of essential skills and understandings can be found wherever educators have discussed and debated which aspects of their disciplines are most important for students to learn in K–12 classrooms. State and local curriculum documents define what the state or district deems to be essential. We believe that teachers must examine, synthesize, evaluate, and use these documents in the ways that best serve their own students in their individual classrooms. These guides are most valuable as parameters or starting points for teacher planning.

For example, consider the "Functions" Standard for grades 9–12 from the National Council of Teachers of Mathematics (Figure 6.3). This standard outlines six essential elements of understanding and using functions in mathematics. These essentials serve as a framework for planning. Decisions about the use of textbooks, demonstrations, classroom activities, and problem sets are all filtered through the six essentials.

FIGURE 6.3. NCTM STANDARD 6: FUNCTIONS

In grades 9–12, the mathematics curriculum should include the continued study of functions so that all students can—

♦ Represent and analyze phenomena with a variety of functions; [*skill*]

♦ Represent and analyze relationships using tables, verbal rules, equations, and graphs; [*skill*]

♦ Translate among tabular, symbolic, and graphical representations of functions; [*skill*]

♦ Recognize that a variety of problem situations can be modeled by the same type of function; [*understanding*]

♦ Analyze the effects of parameter changes on the graphs of functions; [*skill*]

And so that, in addition, college-intending students can—

♦ Understand operations on, and the general properties and behavior of, classes of functions. [*understanding*] (NCTM, 1997)

Performance assessment takes time to design and to implement. We believe that this time is well spent, and that this type of assessment has many advantages for teachers and students. We do caution, however, that teachers should focus performance assessment on the kinds of broad, higher-level skills and content that we have discussed. The power of performance assessment to engage students, to increase their learning, and to give teachers an authentic picture of student achievement is maximized when essential skills and understandings are the focus.

COMPONENT 2: THE CRITERIA—WHAT CHARACTERISTICS OF QUALITY IN THE STUDENTS' WORK WILL WE ACCEPT AS EVIDENCE OF THEIR LEARNING?

The criteria and the rubric connect the essential goal with the task students will perform. They articulate clearly what students are expected to know and be able to do. They drive out the ambiguity and secrecy that sometimes characterizes testing. Clear criteria and rubrics create a structure for students to do their best, and for teachers to provide meaningful feedback that improves performance and prompts learning.

In Chapter 5, we discussed the role of criteria in designing open-ended questions. Teachers who are developing criteria for performance assessments will find that the process is the same as for essay tests. To review: Criteria answer the question, "What evidence will I accept that the student has achieved this goal?" Another way of asking the question is, "What does this skill look like when it is done well?"

Criteria define the goal, focusing both teacher and student attention on the essential elements of what students will know and be able to do. For example, the following criteria could define the goal "Organize and display data using a graph":

1. Select a type of graph or chart that is suited to the data being organized.
2. Make a complete graph; include all the component parts.
3. Transfer information to the graph accurately.
4. Use a graphing utility to create a graph that is organized, neat, and easy to read.
5. Describe the trends, patterns, or relationships that are shown in the graph; summarize the information communicated in the graph.

The quality of a set of criteria can have a major impact, either positive or negative, on instruction and learning. Solid, clear criteria provide students a way of understanding where they are headed, what the goal "looks like," and where they should aim their efforts. Vague or confusing criteria have the opposite effect. Students may spend their time and effort trying to figure out what the criteria mean (i.e., reading the teacher's mind) rather than improving the quality of their work. Teachers might use the checklist in Figure 6.4 (p. 98) to review their criteria before presenting them to students.

FIGURE 6.4. CRITERIA REVIEW CHECKLIST

☐ Are the criteria stated in language that students can understand?

☐ Taken together, do the criteria give students a clear picture of my expectations?

☐ Have I used, discussed, and given models of the criteria during my instruction, so that students understand what the criteria really mean?

☐ Are the criteria closely tied to the goal? If students accomplish everything on the list of criteria, will they have accomplished the essential goal?

☐ Are these criteria unambiguous enough to be used reliably?

After criteria are set and the teacher is confident about their quality, they can then serve as the starting point for the development of a rubric. Although we have said that the design of performance assessments often does not occur in a linear, step-by-step fashion, it *is* important that criteria be established before rubrics are designed.

COMPONENT 3: THE RUBRIC—HOW WILL THE STUDENTS' WORK BE SCORED OR GRADED?

The rubric sets levels of performance for the skill, understanding, or task being assessed. What distinguishes a rubric from a simple grading scale is that the rubric not only *sets*, but also *describes* levels of performance. The rubric does the very important job of letting students know what their score or grade *means*. In Chapter 5, we described how teachers might develop rubrics (or scoring guides) for open-ended questions, compared holistic and analytic rubrics, and listed some of the features that teachers should try to "build in" when designing scoring guides. Rubrics developed for performance assessments should have all these same characteristics. In this section, we discuss rubrics in more depth and give examples of rubrics to accompany performance assessment tasks.

Rubrics take a variety of forms. There are several decisions to be made about the rubric's structure during the design process. Figure 6.5 serves as a guide for this decision making.

FIGURE 6.5. RUBRIC DESIGN PROCESS

Question 1:
What will the rubric be designed to score?

A rubric for a skill or a product is designed to score a skill that is learned and assessed *over time,* or a product that students will do *more than once.*

A task-specific rubric is designed to score a specific task that students will do within the context of a single unit or course.

Examples:

♦ Conduct research

♦ Write persuasively

♦ Play the clarinet

♦ Use math to solve problems

♦ Work productively in a group

Examples:

♦ Make a travel brochure on an European country

♦ Make a model of a cell

♦ Present a dramatic interpretation of a major event of the civil rights movement

♦ Analyze a set of data using measures of central tendency

Question 2:
How will the rubric be structured?

Holistic rubrics are structured so that the student receives one score or grade for the entire task.

Analytic rubrics are structured so that the student receives a score or grade for each component of the task.

As the first question in Figure 6.5 suggests, designers of rubrics must first decide what the rubric will be used to score. With their identified learning goals to guide them, teachers may decide that they want to develop one rubric that can be used again and again as students develop a complex skill over time. This would be a *rubric for a skill or product*, and it may be structured either holistically or analytically. Teachers often develop this kind of rubric to correlate with an essential skill or with a type of product that is important to the course. Although the specifics of the task may change, the basic rubric is used each time. The advantage of this is that students can use their scores and feedback from one task to help them improve before they perform that task again.

An English teacher, for example, may require students to write several literary analyses during the semester or year. The rubric for this skill would address all the essential elements of a literary analysis, but would not address the piece of literature specifically. Goals unique to a particular piece of literature would be "attached" to the rubric each time or assessed using another method, such as a controlled-response test. The same "literary analysis rubric," used at the end of each unit of study, would provide students with consistent expectations that they could work toward over time. These expectations might include:

♦ Sunnarizing the author's message.

♦ Analyzing the plot.

♦ Analyzing the characters' relationships and motivations.

♦ Describing how the setting influences the plot and characters.

♦ Inferring how the time and culture in which the author lived are reflected in the text.

A *task-specific rubric*, as its name suggests, is designed to rate, either holistically or analytically, student work on a single performance task. This rubric would refer to particular aspects of the task and could not be applied to other activities. The primary advantage of a task-specific rubric is that the student can receive very focused feedback. When task-specific rubrics are available during instruction, they help guide students' work. The disadvantage of a task-specific rubric, of course, is that a separate rubric must be designed for each performance assessment. Unless students are going to do the very same task repeatedly, they will only be scored on this rubric once.

For example, in an English class, students might be asked to write a literary analysis of *Romeo and Juliet*. A rubric developed for this assignment might include the criteria for literary analysis found in the more general rubric, but it would also contain elements specific to this play. For example, students might be expected to compare characters from *Romeo and Juliet* to parallel characters from *West Side Story*.

The second question that teachers must answer in designing rubrics (see Figure 6.5) is "How will the rubric be structured?" Rubrics may be either holistic or analytic in structure. These two rubric formats were described in some detail in Chapter 5. To review: A holistic approach combines all the criteria into each level of the rubric; the student receives one score on the task, reflecting the student's overall performance. An analytic rubric is used to score the student's work on a set of components, most often yielding one score for each criterion.

To understand how teachers go about designing rubrics, consider the following illustration. Suppose a teacher plans to have students give oral presentations once each grading period. The topics will reflect the units being studied at the time. The teacher wishes to design a rubric that will help students learn the components of a quality presentation. The teacher also wants to keep the criteria consistent from one quarter to the next, so that students have opportunities to improve from the beginning to the end of the year. Therefore, this will be a *rubric for a skill or product*, the skill being oral presentation. The teacher begins with the criteria that the teacher has established for quality presentations:

♦ Key content is included and is accurate.

♦ Presentation is well organized, easy to follow.

♦ Presentation is easy for audience to see and hear.

♦ Presenter uses expression and communicates interest/enthusiasm about the topic.

♦ Presenter controls body movement, posture, and mannerisms, and maintains eye contact with audience.

Suppose the teacher chooses a holistic rubric with four levels of performance. The teacher would start by embedding the five criteria listed above into a "meets expectations" level of the rubric. (It might have another label, such as "proficient," "satisfactory," "good," or "passing.") This level of the rubric is for work that shows solid evidence of all the criteria. Notice how, in the partially completed rubric in Figure 6.6 (p. 102), the "meets expectations" level is matched to the five criteria above. Also notice that the teacher has left room for one level of performance *above* "meets expectations," to describe work that surpasses the expectations described in the criteria.

FIGURE 6.6. RUBRIC FOR AN ORAL PRESENTATION: STEP I

Exceeds Expectations	
Meets Expectations	Key content is accurate, and is organized into a presentation that is easy to follow. The audience can hear and see the presenter, as well as any visual aids used. The presenter keeps the audience's attention by maintaining eye contact and using expression. There are no aspects of the presenter's "body language" that distract the audience.
Partially Meets Expectations	
Does Not Meet Expectations	

The next challenge for the teacher is to write descriptors for oral presentations that exceed expectations, those that partially meet expectations, and those that do not meet expectations at all. The best way we have found to develop these levels of the rubric is to examine many pieces of student work, looking for common patterns of performance. In fact, a rubric can be built directly from a collection of student work if the designer is confident that the collection is representative of a typical group of students. In the case of our oral presentations rubric, this means observing many student presentations and noting characteristics of presentations that caused them to stand out as exemplary. We would track the ways in which other presentations tended to fall short of meeting the criteria, and let our rubric reflect these as well.

Our experience working with teachers suggests that using the characteristics of actual student work to describe levels of student performance is extremely valuable. It maximizes the quality of the resulting rubric while providing insight into the characteristics of student work. When teachers can begin with a collection of written work or other student products, we suggest that they sort the work into two groups—one group that meets expectations and one that does not. Having done this, teachers will often look at the work in the "meets expectations" pile and note that a few of these papers or projects actually go beyond expectations in some way. As one teacher said to us, "I feel guilty giving an A to this kid along with the others; his work outshines the other papers in this pile, but they are good solid papers that met all the criteria." The characteristics of these "above-and-beyond" papers will form the description of the "exceeds expectations" level of the rubric (see Figure 6.7).

Likewise, when teachers review the student work in the "does not meet expectations" pile, they often feel compelled to divide this work into two smaller groups. Some teachers we know have termed these the "almost there" and the "not there at all" groups. For many teachers, these seem to be naturally occurring groups. There are students who are making good progress in meeting the criteria but who have not yet mastered them, and there are those who have barely begun or have made little or no attempt to complete the task. In our sample rubric, these two groups form the "partially meets expectations" and "does not meet expectations" levels of the rubric (Figure 6.7).

FIGURE 6.7. RUBRIC FOR AN ORAL PRESENTATION: STEP II

Exceeds Expectations	Content is accurate and well organized, and may include evidence of research that is more detailed or in-depth than the assignment required. The presentation is easy to see and hear, and may include unusually effective visual aids. The presenter keeps the audience's attention, and may engage them with a particularly interesting or creative approach.
Meets Expectations	Key content is accurate, and organized into a presentation that is easy to follow. The audience can hear and see the presenter, as well as any visual aids used. The presenter keeps the audience's attention by maintaining eye contact and using expression. There are no aspects of the presenter's "body language" that distract the audience.
Partially Meets Expectations	Key content is accurate but may not be organized in a way that makes the presentation easy to follow. The presentation may be difficult to see or hear, may not hold the audience's attention, or the presenter's mannerisms or body movements may be distracting.
Does Not Meet Expectations	The presentation is not well prepared. Key content is inaccurate or missing. The presentation is difficult to see or hear, or hard to follow.

When teachers can sort and discuss student work—especially when they do so with colleagues—their rubrics can accurately match the patterns in student performance they are likely to see. Often, however, teachers are designing rubrics to be used for the first time, and a body of student work is not available. In these cases, we recommend that teachers rely on experience to make their "best guess" regarding the other levels of the rubric, and that they be prepared to make revisions after its first use. We know that as teachers examine set after set of student work, they find ways to refine their rubrics. Whether the teacher is using student work samples or a "best guess" to develop the other levels of the rubric, all the descriptors must connect directly to the criteria. Figure 6.7 shows our oral presentations rubric completed, including the remaining three levels.

Another way to organize this same information in a more analytic rubric is to assign points to each of the criteria and rate them separately. Such a rubric might look like the one in Figure 6.8.

FIGURE 6.8. ANALYTIC RUBRIC FOR AN ORAL PRESENTATION

	1 Below	2 Almost meets	3 Meets	4 Exceeds
• Key content is included and is accurate.				
• Presentation is well organized, easy to follow.				
• Presentation is easy for audience to see and hear.				
• Presenter uses expression and maintains eye contact.				
• Presenter controls body movement, posture, and mannerisms.				

Most students will make repeated oral presentations in various classes during the course of their school careers. By collaborating to create criteria for this skill, a group of teachers from the same grade-level team, department, or school could create consistent expectations for oral presentations. As students' skills become more sophisticated, the criteria could be expanded as needed.

Very often teachers will discover that their colleagues are working with students on similar skills but do not have the same expectations for student performance. Looking at this situation from a student's perspective, it is easy to see how learning could be inhibited. For example, suppose that a ninth-grade student has classes with four different teachers each day, and each of these classes involves periodic writing assignments. Each teacher has definite expectations for quality ninth-grade writing, but the four sets of expectations differ! The student suffers in two ways. First, the student must constantly adjust his or her work to fit these varying definitions of quality—the target moves several times a day! Second, as the student focuses more on getting his or her writing "the way the teacher wants it" than on progressing toward a consistent set of expectations, the student's skills are unlikely to improve in any substantive way.

When consistent expectations exist in areas such as writing, speaking, research, or learning behaviors, teachers can articulate these expectations through rubrics that apply across departments and grade levels. These rubrics reinforce the expectations for quality work and give teachers a tool for consistent communication with students, parents, and colleagues.

Most schools have schoolwide goals for student learning that are developed either in school improvement teams or through some other mechanism. We have found that schoolwide discussion of what constitutes "success" for students is a powerful tool for these school-improvement efforts. Collaboratively developed criteria and rubrics give the school a mechanism for focusing attention on a specific area and assuring that expectations are consistent and well articulated. Because rubrics are used to score student work, they also serve as a measurement tool, enabling the faculty to assess the progress made by students over time.

Consider the story of a school that chose "helping students produce quality writing" as a school-improvement goal. In this school, the writing focus began with rubric development, primarily by the English department. English teachers worked together—comparing, negotiating, and revising their own expectations for student writers—until they agreed on a set of criteria for each grade level. Because the school was concerned with writing not just in English class, but across the curriculum, it was important that teachers in other disciplines be able to support the writing focus. These teachers were concerned primarily with their own content and felt comfortable assessing it, but for the most part, they had not worked with the English curriculum and had little or no familiarity with anyone else's expectations for writing. Teachers of science, physical education, math, and other subjects were willing (some of them even eager) to support the "writing across the curriculum" goal, but they needed a clear picture of the criteria for writing at each grade level. The criteria developed by the English teachers were shared with other departments. Some provided input and suggested revisions that would make the criteria a better "fit" for specific types of writing in their content areas. With English teachers taking the lead, groups of faculty members used the criteria for each grade level to design rubrics that could serve as a basis for scoring various kinds of writing, across the curriculum.

Teachers were able to set aside planning time for meeting across departments in small groups, working with one or two colleagues to practice scoring student writing, or reviewing their writing assignments with one of the English teachers. Because the school used a block schedule, these planning periods were long enough to have the substantive discussion required for this kind of collaborative work. The school administration supported the effort by devoting faculty meeting time to the project and by providing substitutes occasionally to allow teachers extended time during the school day to work together. Through this process, teachers strengthened their professional relationships with each other, learned more about expectations and instruction in other departments, and created a collaborative model that can be used in the future to work toward other schoolwide goals.

One concern that we hear about using rubrics to score student work is that rubrics are time-consuming for teachers to design and apply. It is true that crafting a rubric requires careful thinking about student performance as well as about how to clearly describe levels of performance on a complex task or skill. Rubrics generally go through several revisions, and the process (particularly when a group of teachers collaborate) can indeed be lengthy. However, the conversation about characteristics of student work and how those characteristics translate into levels of performance is a valuable one. Many teachers say that the *process* of rubric design is as helpful to them as the final product. Block scheduling facilitates this process by providing extended periods of time for teachers to plan collaboratively.

When it comes to the actual scoring of student work, many teachers believe that applying a rubric will take significantly longer than checking the answers on a controlled-response test. In some cases, this is true. However, there are many situations in which the scoring is done *as the student is performing the task,* which would normally be during the regular class period. The student gets immediate feedback and the teacher doesn't go home weighed down with a load of papers to grade!

In other cases, the teacher will have a product for scoring outside of class. If the rubric was introduced early and referred to throughout the instructional process, then the student has had opportunities to adjust and improve the project *before* turning it in. In addition, the teacher has seen the project as the student has worked on it and already knows many of its characteristics. All these factors make the scoring process more efficient. To keep the scoring process as reliable and fair as possible, we recommend that teachers use the scoring suggestions outlined in Chapter 5.

COMPONENT 4: THE TASK—WHAT ACTIVITY OR PROJECT WILL THE STUDENTS UNDERTAKE TO DEMONSTRATE THEIR LEARNING?

The task, the fourth and final component of a performance assessment, is the actual activity students will undertake. This is the students' avenue for showing evidence of their learning. The task is generally based on a *product,* a *performance,* or a combination of product and performance. A *product* is a concrete piece of work submitted as evidence of the learning; this could be a document, such as a research paper or newspaper article, but it may take other forms, such as a display or model. When the task is a *performance,* students are observed and scored as they demonstrate their skill and knowledge. It is easy to imagine scoring student performances in areas of the curriculum such as performing arts and physical education, but teachers interested in performance assessment have discovered that there are ample opportunities for student performance in almost all areas of the curriculum—lab demonstrations in science, debates in social studies, dramatic readings in English. Figure 6.9 (p. 108) provides examples of products and performances that could be linked to a rubric and used to assess student learning.

The design of assessment tasks, whether they are products or performances, is a perfect opportunity for teachers to exercise their creative thinking and innovative ideas. Unlike most traditional testing, performance assessment challenges teachers to come up with tasks that are engaging enough to capture student interest. Performance tasks can take so many different forms that teachers can be just as creative in crafting assessments as they are in designing their lessons. Imagine student assessments such as these:

♦ Interview a war veteran. Tell the class about the background of the person you interviewed, and show the videotape of your interview to the class. Point out information in the tape that helps answer the questions on your interview guide.

♦ Assume that you are an office manager. Create an evaluation tool for employees in the office. The performance evaluation you create must emphasize the important skills and behaviors of clerical staff.

♦ Design a series of at least six "circuit training" activities. The complete circuit must include activities to develop (a) strength, (b) endurance, and (c) flexibility.

Although we encourage teachers to be innovative and imaginative in designing tasks, important issues must be considered in order to assure their quality. The questions in Figure 6.10 (p. 109) can serve as guidelines to help teachers design tasks that are engaging and that also yield meaningful information about student learning of essential skills and knowledge. Performance tasks that meet these guidelines are likely to be useful and effective, as long as they are well matched to the instruction that has occurred and to the rubrics that accompany them.

FIGURE 6.9. EXAMPLES OF RUBRIC-LINKABLE
PRODUCTS AND PERFORMANCES

Product	*Performance*
Use design software to create a blueprint for a single-family dwelling.	Use design software to create a blueprint for a single-family dwelling, present the design and explain the process used to create the design.
Develop a position paper on a controversial issue.	Participate in a debate of a controversial issue. Present your position and offer rebuttals to the opposition.
Design and conduct a scientific experiment. Write a lab report of the results.	Conduct a scientific experiment. Present your procedures and discuss your findings. Be prepared to respond to questions from the audience.
Create a chart that outlines safety guidelines for use in a science laboratory, a food preparation area, a health clinic, or a technology lab.	Demonstrate the procedures for handling lab equipment, a commercial food processor, an autoclave, or a digital camera.
Solve a given problem.	Solve a given problem. Teach a selected group how to solve the problem.
Prepare an audiotape of a musical selection.	Perform a live musical selection.
Paint a picture of a landscape.	Demonstrate a technique for creating depth of field in paintings.
Choreograph a dance for a musical selection.	Choreograph and perform a dance for a musical selection.

FIGURE 6.10. GUIDELINES FOR DESIGNING ENGAGING TASKS

♦ **Is this task worth doing?**

By performing this task, will students really demonstrate what they know and can do? Does this task get *directly* at the essential skills and content to be assessed?

♦ **Is it challenging?**

Will this task require students to go beyond recalling content and replicating skills, stretching them to higher levels of thinking?

♦ **Is it balanced?**

Is the task clear and unambiguous, and at the same time open-ended enough to allow students to respond in a variety of ways?

♦ **Is it authentic?**

Does the task at least approximate something that a person might do in the world outside of school? Are students solving the kinds of problems one might find in a real situation?

♦ **Is it valid for the criteria that have been set?**

Is there a close match between the task and the criteria? If students do this task as it is designed, will they be demonstrating all the criteria?

♦ **Is it fair and equitable?**

Is the task free of bias in its content? Is it equally accessible to all students in the event that special materials or resources are needed?

♦ **Is it reasonable?**

Is this a task that is practical for classroom use?

INTEGRATING PERFORMANCE ASSESSMENT AND INSTRUCTION

Understanding that valid assessment can take place within the context of instruction can be challenging for teachers who are accustomed to separating instruction from assessment. Ask a group of teachers about the practice of teaching during a test and they're likely to say, "That's cheating!" In most schools, teaching and learning take place *until* it is time for the test; then both teaching and learning actions are suspended until test taking is complete. We encourage practices that embed performance assessment in the instructional process, but that still challenge students and do not sacrifice assessment validity to do so. We believe that students who are working to develop a product or performance that is going to be scored *should* receive feedback and guidance as they are working, so that they can improve their work along the way.

For example, suppose a teacher is teaching a unit on simple and compound machines. The performance task is presented to the students on the first day of the unit:

> Design and construct a compound machine to extract toothpaste from a tube. Use as many simple machines (and as many *different* simple machines) as possible in your device.

With this project in mind, the students begin their study of simple machines. They learn the content—how each simple machine works, what its parts are, and its most common uses. Students have a clear purpose for learning this content, as they will be applying it soon in their projects. Soon after the unit begins, students are asked to begin working on a sketch of their Toothpaste Extractor. Class time is devoted to activities such as these:

- ◆ Use your preliminary sketch to check your design against the criteria on your scoring rubric. If your Toothpaste Extractor were to be judged today, what score would you probably receive and why?

- ◆ Have another student look at your sketch. Ask him or her to identify each of the simple machines that you have included and to tell what its role is in making your device operate. Ask your partner to use the rubric to suggest one improvement you could make to your device.

- ◆ Look at the sketches done by three other students. For each of their plans, identify one positive characteristic of the design that distinguishes it from others. Take this list of three strengths back and look at it beside your own design. Other than duplicating another person's idea, are there ways that you can incorporate these strengths into your own design?

All these ideas guide students to assess their own work in light of the criteria shown in the rubric. Using this feedback, they would make revisions to their sketches. Before they begin to build, the teacher might pose questions to guide students as they turn their sketches into real devices. There might be lessons on measurement, discussions about what kinds of materials will make the devices work best, or "troubleshooting" sessions in which students share their plans and invite the class to identify potential problems. All of these activities help the student create a better product. And, yes, they help him get a better grade—but is this "cheating"? We would assert that these are all valuable *learning* experiences that contribute to students' content knowledge and skill development.

Here are some strategies that teachers can use to embed performance assessment into instructional practice:

♦ **Share criteria with and teach criteria to students.**

Providing students with lists of criteria or scoring rubrics is a necessary piece of performance-based instruction, but it is not usually sufficient. Not every student will immediately understand the criteria or see how to apply them to their own work (McTighe, 1997, pp. 9–10). We absolutely agree with McTighe's assertion that just *informing* students of the criteria—perhaps providing them as a handout or posting them in the classroom—in no way assures that students understand them. Criteria are ideas that must be *taught*, using instructional strategies that will help students understand their meaning.

♦ **Share and discuss models so that students can see examples of quality work.**

One way that learners develop understanding is by analyzing examples and nonexamples of the concepts that they are learning. Even as adults, we often ask for an example when we are faced with a new idea; seeing "what it looks like" gives us a reference point. In the context of performance assessment, this indicates the need for students to see models of quality work. With these models, students can discuss how the work exemplifies the criteria. Students can also benefit from examining work that does not meet the criteria and noticing how it differs from work of higher quality. By making the learning goals clear and concrete for students, these activities help them improve their own performance. For example, a flute student who is working on maintaining pitch might play a series of notes along with a teacher. If the student's pitch is flat, she will be able to hear the difference and adjust her pitch to match the teacher's. Similarly, students might compare such things as writing selections, science project displays, or videos of athletic performance skills to exemplary samples provided by the teacher.

♦ **Point out to students how each learning activity relates to one or more of the criteria and prepares them for the performance task.**

During the course of daily instruction, teachers can help students by frequently referring to the criteria. Whether students are involved in a cooperative learning activity, taking notes on a lecture, participating in a debate, or playing a game, they should always see the connection between their current activity and the criteria. Linking their daily activities to the essential goals not only keeps students "on track" but also helps answer the perennial question, "Why are we doing this?"

♦ **Use the criteria to provide feedback on practice assignments and class activities.**

As students participate in class activities and complete assignments, teachers provide feedback to help them improve their work. This feedback should consistently and repeatedly refer to the criteria, so that students can identify how features and components of their work match the various criteria.

♦ **Give students strategies and time for self-assessment and peer assessment.**

The process of analyzing and assessing their own work and the work of fellow students is a powerful teaching and learning strategy. It helps link the criteria with students' actual work and provides a framework for students to share ideas and feedback with each other. These activities help students develop the thinking skills they need in order to analyze their own output, rather than waiting for a grade from the teacher to determine the quality of the work.

In this chapter, we presented a rationale for the use of performance assessment and described a process for designing performance assessments. We reiterate that performance assessment is unlikely to be a teacher's only assessment tool. Another form of student assessment is more appropriate in many situations. Most instructional units will have quizzes, homework assignments, or perhaps tests embedded in them to check for understanding along the way. The performance task, likely to be more complex and challenging, would probably come at or near the end of the unit and be used to "pull together" the subparts. In other situations, the performance assessment is a long-term task that students work on all the way through the unit—building, revising, and improving it as they hone their skills. We believe that there is a place for performance assessment in every content area at every level, and that the use of quality performance assessment can maximize student learning.

7

COMMUNICATION OF ASSESSMENT DATA

THE IMPORTANCE
OF COMMUNICATION

The analysis of student performance is a process that occurs regularly in the classroom. A teacher who strives to engage students and to involve them in the lesson constantly monitors their progress and their needs. Through this ongoing evaluation, the teacher knows when adjustments are needed in the lesson. Thus, assessment data provide teachers with essential feedback. Assessment data also inform students and their parents, offering evidence of what and how students are learning.

Assessment informs the communication process among students, teachers, and parents. Painting an accurate picture of a student's performance—whether in narratives, conferences, or portfolios—calls for a wide range of assessment strategies. Imagine that assessment in a semester-long course always takes the form of controlled-response tests; the resulting image of student knowledge and skills is limited and possibly even inaccurate. By contrast, consider a course where methods of assessment include tests, products, and performances, perhaps even organized into a portfolio. Here, students have a chance to express themselves in a variety of ways, and the information available creates a rich and detailed picture of student learning.

In this chapter, we discuss three means of communicating the assessment of student achievement: grades, conferences, and portfolios. Block schedules provide the time needed for students to be involved in a variety of assessments, ranging from controlled-response tests to assignments asking students to create a product or demonstrate their knowledge and skills in a performance. As the measures of student achievement expand, so too should the methods of reporting their progress.

THE LIMITATIONS OF GRADES
AS COMMUNICATION TOOLS

A common method of reporting student achievement is to assign numerical values to quiz, test, and homework results, and then to determine the average of these marks. This numerical value is then matched to a letter grade and reported to parents via the report card. Although a familiar practice, the averaging of grades may produce a distorted and incomplete picture of a student's achievement (Canady and Hotchkiss, 1989). As an illustration, imagine that you are planning a trip and need to decide what clothing to pack. You know the high temperatures recorded over the last eight days at your destination. Completion of the exercise in Figure 7.1 illustrates the problems inherent in averaging grades to ascertain a student's acheivement.

FIGURE 7.1. AN EXERCISE IN AVERAGING

Daily High Temperatures in Degrees Fahrenheit

Day 1	Day 2	Day 3	Day 4	Day 5	Day 6	Day 7	Day 8
64	62	56	48	42	40	48	50

♦ What was the average daily high temperature during this period? *(51°F)*

♦ How far did temperatures range from the average? *(+13°F to –11°F)*

♦ Does the high temperature that is reported provide a clear picture of what the day was like?

♦ Does the average daily high temperature provide you with a true understanding of what the eight-day period was like?

♦ If the temperature chart had ended on day 6, would you have accurately predicted the next two days?

♦ To plan for your trip, what other weather factors would need to be considered?

♦ Consider the following words and phrases used to forecast the weather during this same period:
  • Mostly sunny
  • Mostly cloudy
  • Breezy
  • Mild
  • Chilly
  • Heavy rain
  • Patchy fog
  • Blustery

How would this part of the forecast influence your packing decisions?

You may have discovered two things doing the exercise in Figure 7.1. First, if you dressed for the average day, you would be uncomfortable much of the time! The average temperature does not in and of itself represent the temperature for the time period. Second, temperature is not the same as weather; a 50-degree day in a downpour is much different than a 50-degree sunny day!

How might these lessons apply to the averaging of grades as a means of communicating student performance? Figure 7.2 presents questions similar to those you just answered in Figure 7.1, but in the context of grading.

FIGURE 7.2. AVERAGING GRADES

Grade 1	Grade 2	Grade 3	Grade 4	Grade 5	Grade 6	Grade 7	Grade 8
94	92	86	85	80	70	76	80

- What is the average grade? *(82.9)*

- How far did the grades range from this average? *(+11.1 to –12.9)*

- Does the daily grade provide any information regarding the specific strengths or weaknesses of the student?

- Does the average grade provide you with a clear understanding of the student's achievement?

- If the grading chart had ended on day 6, would you have accurately predicted the student's future performance?

- To plan for instruction, what additional information do you need?

- Consider the following words used to describe the student during this grading period:
  - Attentive
  - Focused
  - Sleepy
  - Tardy
  - Absent
  - Confused
  - Hard working

How might this information influence your grading decisions?

The average of the student's scores in Figure 7.2 is 82.9. On a grading scale such as the one below, this student would be assigned a grade of C.

95–100	A
88–94	B
81–87	C
75–80	D
0–74	F

Does this C accurately reflect this student's performance? If it does, then consider the same student in a school where the grading scale is as shown below.

90–100	A
80–89	B
70–79	C
60–69	D
0–59	F

In this school, the student receives a grade of B for the very same scores. In neither instance does the grade provide any information about what the student learned. Just as the average temperature for a series of days does not help us dress for the weather, an average score does not inform us about student learning.

Traditionally, teachers have relied almost exclusively on controlled-response formats, such as multiple-choice and true/false tests. These generally produce numerical scores that are averaged with other numerical scores from homework, quizzes, and other assignments to determine a letter grade. These letters and numbers have little real meaning at best, and at worst can distort a student's performance. If students are to understand and further their learning, they must receive and process more and better feedback.

Furthermore, this feedback should be both *timely* and *specific*. Students should not be kept waiting until the end of the grading period to find out how they are doing. All of us, when learning something new, have wondered, "How am I doing?" We want to know if we are on the right track; we want someone to take away our self-doubt and to assure us that *we can do it*. As educators, we should let this question echo in our heads, as a reminder that students look to us for that same assurance.

Of course it is of very little significance to the learner if the feedback is timely but lacks specificity. Who of us have not received one of those infamous red-inked papers with errors circled and a grade at the top, but with no feedback as to how the "wrong" might be corrected? We know how frustrating and time-consuming it can be to analyze the ink marks to determine what was wrong and figure out how to avoid the mistake in the future. We know, too, how few students are likely to take the initiative and seek out the teacher for more information and guidance.

The giving of number or letter grades can be just as uninformative. As Wiggins (1988) emphasizes, "A grade is usable by students only if the criteria behind it are explicit and put in *descriptive* terms" (p. 24). Students who receive a grade with no specific feedback often think the grade reflects the teacher's like or dislike of the student, rather than the student's performance. Consider the story of a high school mathematics teacher who decided to give stickers to anyone in her class who received an A on a chapter checkup. Imagine her surprise when students began to examine their papers and ask, "Why didn't I get a sticker?" and, more importantly, "What do I need to do to get one?" The same students who, when given a grade, had glanced at their papers before putting (or throwing) them away, now were trying to determine a reason for their "rewards." Does this mean that all secondary teachers should embrace the sticker-giving strategy? No—but it does demonstrate that students have, in a sense, become immune to grades. They may have developed an acceptance of grading practices without developing a true understanding of their meaning.

Canady and Hotchkiss (1989) suggest that teachers need to reflect on grading practices that might be counterproductive for students. Of the dozen practices they identified, we discuss these:

- ♦ Failing to match the testing to teaching
- ♦ Establishing inconsistent criteria
- ♦ Practicing "gotcha" teaching
- ♦ Suggesting that success is unlikely

As we have stated throughout this book, it is of utmost importance that curriculum, instruction *and* assessment be aligned. To accomplish this seamless match, teachers must realize that planning instruction and planning assessments go hand in hand. When teachers know what they expect of students, they can plan for the classroom experiences that will help students reach the stated objectives. When students know *from the beginning* what is expected of them, they are more likely to see the connection between teaching and testing. Practices such as reviewing and discussing the questions at the end of the chapter *before* students begin to read help to focus the students on expectations. An administrator recently commented that one of the best teachers he knows begins the semester by giving students the questions that will be asked on the final examination. In doing so, that teacher defines the instructional objectives and helps students develop a context for the instructional program.

When students understand what is expected of them and learn to use the criteria as benchmarks for measuring their performance, they become involved in the process of self-assessment. Teachers who use these criteria to communicate expectations and to measure performance support the concept of continuous learning. Students can identify where they are in terms of the learning and know *specifically* what they need to do to improve. The teacher acts as a facilitator of learning, working to support and guide the student. Students who view teachers in this role are more likely to ask for assistance and guidance than those who see teachers as judges waiting to dole out rewards and punishments in the form of grades.

Identifying objectives that are clearly defined and establishing consistent criteria help to keep teachers and students "on track." In essence, taking the guesswork out of grading creates a level of trust between teachers and students. Students who know what is expected of them can focus their energies on mastering content and developing skills. When their performance is assessed, they know what is expected; they can trust that there will be no "gotcha" surprises.

Can you remember a time when you and your classmates got together before a test to "figure out" a teacher? Everyone was involved in the guessing game, trying to predict what was important to Mrs. X, or hoping to gain an insight into Mr. Z's testing methods. Friends who had taken the class before were pressed for tips—"Study the captions under the pictures in the text," they said, or "Memorize all the notes written on the board." Behind this effort to uncover the mysteries of the test was a belief that surprises were in store, that teachers were out to "catch" us on something we did not know, rather than providing opportunities for us to show what we did know. "Gotcha" teaching and testing sends a message to students that their success is tenuous. Rather than feeling confident in their ability to succeed, students feel that control lies in the hands of the teacher. When teachers use only one form of assessment, they handicap students by not allowing them to express their knowledge and demonstrate their skills in different ways. Imagine the frustration of knowing that you have difficulty with a certain method of assessment and realizing that this will be the *only* form used in the classroom to measure your achievement! Imagine the disillusionment of having your complex learning experience boiled down to a single number or letter grade!

Just as students need a variety of ways to demonstrate what they have learned, so do teachers need more than a letter or number grade to describe student performance. When teachers expand their assessment strategies to include the range of assessments from controlled-response tests to open-ended essays and performances, they must also examine new methods of communicating the results of student performance.

PORTFOLIOS AS COMMUNICATION TOOLS

Concrete examples of student performance, collected and organized into a portfolio, can serve as the basis for assessment *and* communication. According to Stenmark (1991), a portfolio is an "assessment medium" that serves to "showcase" student work.

> This assessment medium enables students to demonstrate learning and understanding of ideas beyond facts and knowledge. A wide variety of items can be collected to support a broad curriculum. The more open the possibilities, the more useful the portfolio will be. (pp. 35–36)

Stenmark also discusses the value of the portfolio as part of the conversations between teachers, students, and parents. "Having students take portfolios home now and then can open communication and understanding for parents.

Improvement over time can be illustrated and can be a beginning of discussion in conferences" (p. 36).

Rather than speaking in general terms about the student's work, teachers and students can work together to *examine* work samples and to discuss the student's progress toward the learning target. The importance of involving students in communicating about their own skills and abilities cannot be overstated. When students are provided opportunities to be involved in this conversation, they have an active role in their own learning. As they analyze their strengths and weaknesses, they will be in a position to better understand their needs and recognize their accomplishments.

Wolf (1989) compares the students' involvement in the use of portfolios to the construction of "a story—a long term account—of what and how [the students] learn" (p. 38). The elements of a portfolio can be used by the student to recreate for others his process of thinking and learning. We refer to this type of portfolio as a *progress portfolio.*

Picture the student as the storyteller and the elements of the portfolio as the story's illustrations. Items that are to be included in the portfolio must be selected purposefully. The development of the portfolio becomes part of the learning process. Items are revisited, re-created, and redesigned as the student's knowledge and skill increase. Choices are made about what should be discarded and what should remain as learning artifacts. The use of this type of portfolio adds depth to the assessment process. Rather than creating a single product or presenting a final performance, students must analyze the processes of creation, production, and learning in order to create a portfolio that demonstrates progress.

Comprehensive goals for students, such as the four goals identified in the Mathematics Standards of Learning for Virginia Public Schools (Commonwealth of Virginia Board of Education, 1995), provide the "big picture" of a successful math student. To reach these goals, students must do more than memorize facts, rules, and theories. They must use their knowledge of content to reason and solve problems, communicate mathematically, and make "mathematical connections" (p. 3). The development of skills in communication, reasoning, and problem solving is not a finite process that can be assessed by a single test, product, or performance. Student performances must be measured over time in order to determine the progress being made toward the accomplishment of the goals.

Another type of portfolio is what we call a *best works portfolio.* In this case, the portfolio still tells a story, but it is a story of the student's current level of accomplishment rather than one of progress over time. The purpose of this type of portfolio is to showcase the level of work the student can produce. These are like the portfolios that architects, photographers, and a range of professionals use to demonstrate their skills. This collection includes only those pieces that represent the student's view of his or her best work. During the creation of a best works portfolio, students are examining their work and updating it as their knowledge and skills increase. The process of choosing pieces is in itself a valuable learning experience, as it prompts students to seek feedback and to assess their own work. In a portfolio conference, the student's best works stimulate questions from the teacher and/or parents. These questions lead the student to describe his or her learning process; the story is still being told, but in a somewhat different way.

Regardless of which type of portfolio they choose, it is critical that teachers identify the purpose, content, and organization of the portfolio and communicate these clearly to students. For details and guiding questions to aid teachers in portfolio planning, we suggest *Portfolios Plus: A Critical Guide to Alternative Assessment*, by Linda Mabry (1999).

Collecting and organizing work samples gives students the opportunity to review their growth in knowledge and skills. The selected portfolio items help students reflect on the larger learning goals rather than focusing on discrete skills. Teachers can generate questions to help students decide which work samples will become part of their portfolio collection and which will be discarded. These questions, reflecting the instructional goals, can guide the development of the portfolios as well as the conversation that ensues when students share their portfolios with others. Included in Figure 7.3 (p. 124) are examples of the questions teachers might pose to guide students as they develop and later assess their portfolios.

The questions in Figure 7.3 are critical to guiding students' thinking about their portfolios. Questions such as the following could also be part of a portfolio discussion:

- Which is your favorite portfolio piece? What makes it your favorite?

- Which piece are you most proud of and why?

- Which piece was most difficult for you? What made it difficult?

- If you could do this portfolio over again, what would you change? How would it be different?

- If you were to continue to develop this portfolio, what would you want to include?

- Which piece required you to seek the most help from outside sources?

- Which piece required the most time?

- With whom would you share this portfolio (other than your teacher and parents)?

FIGURE 7.3. PORTFOLIO PLANNING AND CONFERENCING

Your portfolio should contain work samples that you can use to demonstrate your knowledge and skills. Think of the items you select as part of a storytelling process. You will use the portfolio to tell a story about what and how you have learned. The following questions are based on classroom goals, objectives, and criteria that should be familiar to you. The questions will be used in conferences where you will be asked to share your portfolio and to explain its development. You may add questions to the list that you wish to include in the discussions.

Questions

1. What are the most important ideas or concepts you have learned? Which portfolio pieces show that you understand these concepts?

2. What are the most important skills you have developed? Which portfolio pieces show that you have mastered these skills?

3. How have your understandings and/or skills changed?

4. How have you used your knowledge and skills to answer questions or to solve problems?

5.

Used well, a student's portfolio is a powerful tool for learning and for communicating about learning. A quality portfolio is not just a folder in which students insert items guided by the teacher's checklist. Rather, the teacher provides feedback and assistance to the student as the student creates the story of his or her learning. The value of a portfolio as a communication tool is perhaps best expressed by Enoch (1995):

> If a picture is worth a thousand words, then a portfolio is worth countless report cards. If we want parents to truly understand the products, the progress, and the thinking processes of children, then portfolios and anecdotal records must be used to transform educational jargon into concrete, visual examples that support and give meaning to the evaluation. Share writing samples, artwork, examples of math projects, science lab reports, and other work from throughout the grading period, as both skill and thought-process development are quite apparent with these types of samples. Consider using more sophisticated portfolios, which can include such items as video or multimedia student reports, audio or video recordings of oral reading, debates, performances, or photographs of student projects. The time spent collecting and organizing portfolios pays great dividends in assisting parents to see (perhaps for the first time) the progress or lack of progress their child is making. Combined with more traditional assessment tools, portfolios help both parents and teachers see a more complete picture of the development of the student. (p. 46)

CONFERENCES WITH PARENTS AND STUDENTS

Conferencing with students and parents should be a natural part of the instruction and assessment process. Unfortunately, this is not always the case. Given the limited amount of time in the school day and the number of students and parents with whom a teacher must interact, it is easy to see why conferencing may not be an instructional priority. Often the idea of conferencing is equated with a back-to-school night "meet and greet" event, an end-of-the-term "report card huddle," or the dreaded "you're-in-trouble-now" discussion. In many cases, rather than facilitating a discussion about the student's performance, the teacher merely presents a progress report.

An effective conference takes time. Have you ever been in the position, as a teacher or parent, to have a parent-teacher conference scheduled for 15 minutes or less? By the time introductions are made, seats are taken, and records or report cards reviewed, the allotted time has elapsed. Rather than a conversation or discussion, what you experienced was more like a "drive-through" handoff of information. Even when conference time is extended to 30 minutes, the clock continues to limit the dialogue. A benefit of the block schedule is the increased amount of time in each planning period. In the past, teachers working in traditional schedules have been lucky to have enough time in their planning period to return a telephone call and visit the restroom before meeting with the next group of students. Teachers working in block schedules have time during a planning period to conduct a conference with students and/or parents, without rushing. An added benefit for teachers working in a 4/4 semester block schedule is the reduced number of students (and parents) with whom they work each semester. When teachers can focus their energies on a smaller group of students, it is more likely that the time devoted to conferencing will increase, and the quality of the interactions with students and parents will improve.

Another benefit of some block scheduling models is that they provide time for teachers to plan with their team. This planning block facilitates an integrated approach to instructional planning, and provides time for a teacher or team of teachers to conference with students and parents. A sample four-block schedule designed for a two-teacher team at the middle school level is shown in Figure 7.4 (Rettig and Canady, 2000, p. 83).

FIGURE 7.4. FOUR-BLOCK SCHEDULE, TWO-TEACHER TEAM

Times	*8:00–8:10*	*Block I 8:10–9:40*	*Block II 9:45–11:15*	*11:20–11:50*	*Block III 11:55–1:25*	*Block IV 1:30–3:00*
Teacher A Language Arts and Social Studies	HR	Group 1 Language Arts	Group 2 Language Arts	Lunch	Social Studies Group 2 (Sem. 1) Group 1 (Sem. 2)	Teachers: Individual and Team Planning Time
Teacher B Math and Science	HR	Group 2 Math	Group 1 Math	Lunch	Science Group 1 (Sem. 1) Group 2 (Sem. 2)	Students: PE and Exploratory Block

Note: This schedule is designed for a two-semester rotation, in which students take one semester each of science and social studies. HR denotes the homeroom period.

SOURCE: Canady, R.L., and Rettig, M.D. (2000). *Scheduling Strategies for Middle Schools.* Larchmont, NY: Eye On Education. Used with permission.

Many scheduling models provide time for collaborative planning and conferencing. For additional middle school models and details about their use, we suggest *Scheduling Strategies for Middle Schools* (2000) by Michael D. Rettig and Robert Lynn Canady. For high school block schedules, consult *Block Scheduling: A Catalyst for Change in High Schools* (1995) by Robert Lynn Canady and Michael D. Rettig.

The conference should be thought of as a *conversation* between teachers, parents, and students. If the conversation is to be effective, there must be interaction among those who are present. Too often, conferences are one-sided, with the teacher in charge of the reporting, while parents and students listen and contribute an occasional question or comment. Generally, the teacher reports *how* the student is doing in class, without focusing on the details of *what* the student has done or is expected to do. Because parents do not have firsthand experience of what has occurred in the classroom, their ability to contribute to this type of discussion is limited. When teachers design conferences around specific performance criteria, they provide opportunities for parents and students to understand not only *how* the student is doing, but *what* the student is doing. This opens the way for a discussion of *why* the student is performing in this manner, a discussion that is likely to provide useful information for the parents and the student. If the conversation is effective, the teacher learns something, too.

Writing as a superintendent of schools and as a parent, Enoch (1995) describes his frustrations with parent-teacher conferences:

> Despite the best intentions of excellent teachers—and in this case, my own sincere desire for meaningful information—I knew that most conferences consist primarily of reviewing a completed report card, with perhaps a computer printout of test scores to refer to. While this exercise is of some value, it gives only limited insight, most of which parents could gain at home by reviewing the same documents themselves. (p. 46)

In Enoch's words, the key to the value of the conference is "progress." He suggests that a discussion of "the degree of progress is at least equal in importance to a grade or mark on a report card" (p. 46).

In preparing for a conference with parents and students, it is helpful to establish a focus for the meeting. When teachers communicate this purpose to students, they can come to the conference prepared to participate in a discussion rather than just receive information. Likewise, sending a letter home to parents to confirm the conference date and to provide a format for your time together helps to prepare the parents for the meeting. Instead of being "in the dark" about the purpose of the meeting, parents feel informed and can arrive better prepared to contribute to the conference. Figure 7.5 is a sample format for a conference notification that could be sent to parents or used as a planning document for telephone reminders.

FIGURE 7.5. SAMPLE CONFERENCE NOTIFICATION FORM

Conference Confirmation

Dear _____,

Thank you for scheduling a time to meet with me to discuss _____'s progress. During the conference we will be examining _____'s work and discussing his/her performance. The conference date, time, and location are listed below.

Please stop by the main office to check in when you arrive.

If you have any questions prior to the conference, you may contact me at _____.

I look forward to seeing you on the _____.

Sincerely,

Conference date:

Time: _____ to _____

Location:

Topics:

Questions/Comments:

Another tool that may help to focus conversations about student performance is the rubric that is being used in the classroom with students. As we discussed in Chapters 5 and 6, a rubric designed to accompany a particular task can outline long-term goals as well as short-term objectives. The established goals and criteria present a clear message to parents about expectations and enable them to understand, support, and extend student learning. Rather than dealing with generalities, jargon, and nebulous comments, parents can examine criteria that establish clear expectations for student performance. This makes it more likely that their questions and comments will move beyond a discussion of *what* is being taught to the *how* and *why* of their child's performance.

The importance of involving students in the conference should not be overlooked. When teachers share the responsibility for the conference planning with students, they encourage self-evaluation on the part of the student. Students may use portfolios or scoring guides to help them illustrate the progress they have made. Even in the absence of a portfolio, students may be asked to develop a conference outline that presents an overview of the topics that will be discussed. This outline can be shared with teachers and parents in order to communicate the purpose of the conference. Questions such as the following could help students to prepare their outlines:

- What are my learning goals?
- What evidence can I present that I have met these goals?
- If there are goals that I have not met, what progress can I demonstrate in these areas?
- What support or help do I need in order to reach my goals?
- What is the accomplishment that I am most proud of, and why?

The most effective conferences involve students in active rather than passive roles. Because students have seldom had the opportunity to participate in the planning of a conference, they will need guidance and feedback in order to design conferences that are meaningful. Helping students develop these communication skills enables them to become participants in a dialog, rather than merely presenters or receivers of reports.

REFERENCES

Bellanca, J. (1990). *The cooperative think tank: Graphic organizers to teach thinking in the cooperative classroom.* Palatine, IL: Skylight Publishing.

Blaz, D. (1998). *Teaching foreign languages in the block.* Larchmont, NY: Eye on Education.

Bloom, B. (Ed.) (1956). *Taxonomy of educational objectives, handbook I.* New York: David McKay Company.

Bransford, J. D. and Stein, B. S. (1984). *The ideal problem solver: A guide for improving thinking, learning, and creativity.* New York: W.H. Freeman.

Canady, R. L. and Hotchkiss, P. R. (1989, September). It's a good score! Just a bad grade. *Phi Delta Kappan, 66*(3), 183–184.

Canady, R. L. and Rettig, M. D. (1995). *Block scheduling: A catalyst for change in high schools.* Larchmont, NY: Eye on Education.

Canady, R. L. and Rettig, M. D. (Eds.) (1996). *Teaching in the block: Strategies for engaging active learners.* Larchmont, NY: Eye on Education.

Cawelti, G. (1994). *High school restructuring: A national study.* Arlington, VA: Educational Research Service.

Commonwealth of Virginia Board of Education. (1995). *Standards of learning for Virginia public schools.* Richmond, VA: Author.

Conti-D'Antonio, M., Bertrando, R., and Eisenberger, J. (1998). *Supporting students with learning needs in the block.* Larchmont, NY: Eye on Education.

Costa, A. L. (Ed.) (1991). *Developing minds: A resource book for teaching thinking.* Alexandria, VA: Association for Supervision and Curriculum Development.

Davidson, N. and Worsham, T. (Eds.) (1992). *Enhancing thinking through cooperative learning.* New York, NY: Teachers College Press.

Day, T. (1995, April). New class on the block. *The Science Teacher,* 28–30.

Eggen, P. and Kauchak, D. (1996). *Strategies for teachers: Teaching content and thinking skills.* Boston, MA: Allyn and Bacon.

Enoch, S. W. (1995, March 22). Taking charge of the parent-teacher conference. *Education Week,* 46, 48.

Fogarty, R. and Bellanca, J. (1989). *Patterns for thinking, patterns for transfer.* Palatine, IL: IRI Group.

Gall, M. D. and Rhody, T. (1987). Review of research on questioning techniques. In W. W. Wilen (Ed.), *Questions, questioning techniques, and effective teaching.* Washington, DC: National Education Association.

Gerking, J. (1995, April). Building block schedules. *The Science Teacher,* 23–27.

Goodlad, J. (1994). *What schools are for?* Bloomington, IN: Phi Delta Kappa Educational Foundation.

Gunter, M. A., Estes, T. H. and Schwab, J. (1995). *Instruction, a models approach.* Boston, MA: Allyn and Bacon.

Guskey, T.R. (1997). *Implementing mastery learning.* Belmont, CA: Wadsworth.

Haladyna, T. (1994). *Developing and validating multiple-choice test items.* Hillsdale, NJ: Lawrence Erlbaum Associates.

Herman, J. L. (1992, August). Accountability and alternative assessment: Research and development issues. Los Angeles, CA: National Center for Research on Evaluation, Standards, and Student Testing (CRESST), Graduate School of Education, University of California.

Herman, J. L., Aschbacher, P. R., and Winters, L. (1992). *A practical guide to alternative assessment.* Alexandria, VA: Association for Supervision and Curriculum Development.

Hyerle, D. (1996). *Visual tools for constructing knowledge.* Alexandria, VA: Association for Supervision and Curriculum Development.

Johnson, D. W. and Johnson, R. T. (1992). *Creative controversy: Intellectual challenge in the classroom.* Edina, MN: Interaction Book Company.

Johnson, D. W., Holubec, E. J. and Johnson, R. T. (1988). *Cooperation in the classroom.* Edina, MN: Interaction Book Company.

Johnson, D. W., Johnson R. T., and Holubec, E. J. (1994). *Cooperative learning in the classroom.* Alexandria, VA: Association for Supervision and Curriculum Development.

Kagan, S. (1994). *Cooperative learning.* San Clemente, CA: Kagan Cooperative Learning.

Kemp, J. E., Morrison, G. R., and Ross, S. M. (1998). *Designing effective instruction.* Upper Saddle River, NJ: Prentice-Hall.

Mabry, L. (1999). *Portfolios plus: A critical guide to alternative assessment.* Thousand Oaks, CA: Corwin Press.

Margulies, N. (1991). *Mapping inner space.* Tucson, AZ: Zephyr Press.

Marzano, R. J. and Kendall, J. S. (1996). *Designing standards-based districts, schools, and classrooms.* Alexandria, VA: Association for Supervision and Curriculum Development.

McTighe, J. (1997, January). What happens between assessments? *Educational Leadership,* 6–12.

Morgan, N. and Saxton, J. (1991). *Teaching, questioning and learning.* New York: Routledge, Chapman and Hall.

National Assessment of Educational Progress Mathematics Consensus Project (1996). *Mathematics Framework for the 1996 and 2000 National Assessment of Educational Progress.* Washington, DC: National Assessment Governing Board, US Department of Education.

National Council of Teachers of Mathematics. (1989). *Curriculum and evaluation standards for school mathematics.* Reston, VA: Author.

National Council of Teachers of Mathematics (1997, July). *Fostering algebraic and geometric thinking: Selections from the NCTM standards.* Reston, VA: Author.

Newmann, F. M. (1991). Promoting higher order thinking in social studies: Overview of a study of 16 high school departments. *Theory and Research in Social Education, 19*(4), 324–340.

Popham, W. J. (1999). *Classroom assessment: What teachers need to know.* Boston, MA: Allyn and Bacon.

Rettig, M. D. and Canady, R. L. (2000). *Scheduling strategies for middle schools.* Larchmont, NY: Eye on Education.

Rowe, M. B. (1974). Relation of wait time and rewards to the development of language, logic, and fate control: Part one—Wait time. *Journal of Research in Science Teaching, 11,* 81–94.

Salvaterra, M. and Adams, D. (1995, November). Departing from tradition: Two schools' stories. *Educational Leadership,* 24–27.

Sizer, T. R. (1992). *Horace's school: Redesigning the American high school.* New York: Houghton Mifflin.

Stenmark, J. K. (Ed.) (1991). *Mathematics assessment: Myths, models, good questions, and practical suggestions.* Reston, VA: National Council of Teachers of Mathematics.

Stiggins, R. J. (1997). *Student-centered classroom assessment.* Upper Saddle River, NJ: Merrill.

Strebe, J. (1996). The collaborative classroom. In R.L. Canady and M.D. Rettig (Eds.), *Teaching in the block: Strategies for engaging active learners.* Larchmont, NY: Eye on Education.

Tanner, B. (1996). *Perceived staff development needs of teachers in high schools with block schedules.* Unpublished doctoral dissertation, University of Virginia.

Targuin, P. and Walker, S. (1997). *Creating success in the classroom! Visual organizers and how to use them.* Englewood, CO: Teachers Ideas Press.

Weinstein, C. and Mayer, R. (1986). The teaching of learning strategies. In M. Whittrock (Ed.), *The handbook of research on teaching.*

Wiggins, G. P. and McTighe, J. (1998) *Understanding by design.* Alexandria, VA: Association for Supervision and Curriculum Development.

Wilen, W. W. (1991). *Questioning skills for teachers.* Washington, DC: National Education Association.

Wolf, D. P. (1989, April). Portfolio assessment: Sampling student work. *Educational Leadership,* 35–39.

NOTES

NOTES

NOTES

NOTES

NOTES

NOTES

NOTES

NOTES

NOTES

NOTES

NOTES

NOTES